PERFORMANCE
OF A LIFETIME

BY FRED NEWMAN:

Other books

Unscientific Psychology: A Cultural-Performatory Approach to Understanding Human Life
co-author, Lois Holzman; in press

Let's Develop! A Guide to Continuous Personal Growth
with Phyllis Goldberg

Lev Vygotsky: Revolutionary Scientist
co-author, Lois Holzman

The Myth of Psychology

Plays

Billie & Malcolm: A Demonstration

Carmen's Community

Dead as a Jew (Zion's Community)

Left of the Moon

Lenin's Breakdown
co-author, Dan Friedman

Mr. Hirsch Died Yesterday

Off-Broadway Melodies of 1592

Outing Wittgenstein

Sally and Tom (The American Way)

Still on the Corner

The Store: One Block East of Jerome

What is to be Dead? (Philosophical Scenes)

Performance of a Lifetime

of a Lifetime

A PRACTICAL-PHILOSOPHICAL
GUIDE TO THE JOYOUS LIFE

FRED NEWMAN
WITH PHYLLIS GOLDBERG

CASTILLO INTERNATIONAL • NEW YORK

The people whose situations, stories, and relationships are described in this book are fictional characters based on composites of actual patients in Dr. Newman's social therapy practice.

Castillo International, Inc.
500 Greenwich Street, Suite 201
New York, New York 10013

Library of Congress Catalog Number: 96-83502

Newman, Fred
Performance of a Lifetime: A Practical-Philosophical Guide
to the Joyous Life

ISBN 0-9628621-7-7

BOOK AND COVER DESIGN BY DAVID NACKMAN AND DIANE STILES

00 99 98 97 96   5 4 3 2 1

Manufactured in the United States of America

CONTENTS

Performance of a Lifetime is dedicated to my dearest friends, Gabrielle (Rie) Kurlander and Jacqueline (Jackie) Salit, with whom I live in the joyous zone that is our shared history and society.

ACKNOWLEDGMENTS

Many, many people are included in the ensemble that created *Performance of a Lifetime.* In particular I want to thank the members of the philosophy course that I regularly teach at the East Side Institute for Short Term Psychotherapy, who spiritedly take part in the peculiarly joyous activity of performing philosophizing; Chris Helm and Karen Steinberg, my teaching assistants, who do an excellent job of producing and helping me to direct that performance; and Mark Balsam, Don Hulbert, and Susan Santaniello, who transcribed the class discussions with utmost patience and care.

A triad of doctors, three of my closest colleagues and friends, generously contributed their expertise: Dr. Dan Friedman, a playwright and theatre historian who is the dramaturg of the Castillo Theatre, has taught me a great deal about the history of performance; Dr. Lois Holzman, a distinguished scholar and very gifted teacher who is the director of the Barbara Taylor School in Brooklyn, New York, has taught me about many things, including learning; and Dr. Susan Massad, the director of ambulatory care at Long Island

College Hospital in Brooklyn, a most compassionate and intelligent physician, has taught me much about health.

Kim Svoboda, my wonderfully versatile assistant, was on hand at every stage to do with skill and verve whatever had to be done.

My thanks to a most skilled, dedicated, and productive production team: Diane Stiles, production manager extraordinaire, a postmodern Renaissance woman who does so many things so well; Jessica Massad, the production coordinator, who did her job — making sure that the rest of us did ours — with understanding and grace; David Nackman, the enormously talented designer (and performer) who with Diane gave form to the substance of *Performance*; Chris Street, the tireless typesetter who made it all materialize; and Margo Grant, who proofread with her usual diligence and good humor.

A PREFACE BY PHYLLIS

As Fred and I were completing *Performance of a Lifetime* I found myself thinking about what you, our readers, might be expecting from this "sequel" to *Let's Develop!* It would be natural to assume that *Performance* is simply more of *Develop!* — and I wondered if you'd be pleasantly surprised or somewhat disappointed to discover that we've written a very different kind of book this time around. While the two certainly bear a family resemblance to one another (to borrow a phrase from Ludwig Wittgenstein, Fred's favorite philosopher), they each speak in a particular tone of voice; they each have their own style; they each pursue separate ambitions.

When I mentioned this to Fred, he had the idea that you might like to know how I see the difference between *Let's Develop!* and *Performance of a Lifetime* from my somewhat peculiar point of view as both an outsider (I'm neither a therapist nor a philosopher) and an insider (I've been writing about therapy and philosophy with Fred for the last 17 years).

To me, *Let's Develop!* is like a map that you look at to find out how you can go from here (where you are now) to here (where you want to be). It's designed to help you to live developmentally, given that you're living in our particular society at this particular moment. As a social therapist, Fred doesn't provide you with answers or solutions. Rather, he teaches you how to ask the development question in every situation — which makes it more likely that you'll keep coming up with answers that can lead to your continued personal growth.

Performance of a Lifetime is much more like a poem which takes you by surprise, to a place that perhaps you've never even imagined — what some people think of as the spiritual dimension of human life. For as Fred tries to show in this book, "you" and "I" aren't simply transients who happen to be staying at a temporary societal address during a stopover between birth and death; we also reside, timelessly, in history. Yet many of us tend to be unaware that we belong in both society and history, and so we're unable to experience the joy of hanging out at the intersection where they meet. Fred believes that philosophizing can remind us of our historicalness, and so point us toward that out-of-the-way joyous place.

Performance is a philosophical guide to living joyously, given that we live simultaneously in history and society. Fred's not concerned to tell you what solutions the great philosophers have come up with to this paradoxical existential situation of ours, which they tend to regard as a dilemma or a crisis. Rather, like a theatre director, he's showing you how to perform philosophizing — to ask big questions about little things that may not have any answers — which makes it more likely that you'll be able to see yourself as who you are historically, and come to experience the joy of being and seeing yourself.

It seems to me that *Performance of a Lifetime* is a "harder" book than *Let's Develop!* — which isn't terribly surprising. After all, in our culture it's even more difficult (and looked upon as more weird) for people to live joyously than it is for us to live developmentally. I definitely found *Performance* harder to write.

When Fred asked me to write *Let's Develop!* with him, it was as if he had suggested that we take a walk together. *I'd love to!* I said right away. We walked and talked our way through *Let's Develop!* pretty easily. And although we occasionally climbed higher up than I was used to, so that I got a little out of breath, it never occurred to me that I might not be able to make it.

The writing of *Performance* was a very different story. It was as if Fred had invited me to dance a ballet with him; at first I was much too embarrassed, self-conscious and inhibited to take a step. Having started out life as a "smart little girl," for a long time I thought I needed to know everything. A little later on there was a relatively brief moment when I actually believed I did (that's the myth of Sociology, fortified with youthful arrogance). Now that I've grown up, wanting to have all the answers strikes me as a childish hobby — like collecting baseball cards or bottle tops — and not terribly interesting. Still, I haven't quite lost the habit of assuming that I prefer to do what I already know how to do. My first response to Fred's invitation to write a philosophy book with him was: *I can't! I'm too clumsy and awkward. I don't know how. I don't have the right costume. I'll look ridiculous. You're the philosopher,* I told him. *I'll just stand here and watch.*

As you can see, I did eventually become Fred's partner in the dance of *Performance* — because when I actually thought about it, I realized that the best times of my life have come about as a consequence of my saying yes to doing things that didn't seem to be "me" at all. So I climbed onto the stage and joined him in a performance of philosophizing — clumsily, without knowing how, and no doubt looking quite ridiculous. It's been a strenuous, occasionally tedious, profoundly joyous experience. And now I'd like to invite you to come up here and perform philosophizing with us — there's plenty of room for everyone who wants to dance, and you can come as you are.

— Phyllis Goldberg
New York City

PERFORMANCE
OF A LIFETIME

ME 'N' PHILOSOPHY:
A PERSONAL
INTRODUCTION

I write this lengthy and, I fear, sometimes inaccessible and obscure introduction to present myself to you as a former professional philosopher who has come to believe fervently that everyone (ordinary people) seeking to live developmentally and joyously needs to be engaged in the ongoing *activity of philosophizing*.

As I see it, the classical discipline of Philosophy (with a big "P") died (or has come close to dying) during the last half century. A principal "attending physician," at once compassionate and merciless, was the extraordinary Viennese thinker Ludwig Wittgenstein (1889-1951). The death of Philosophy as a system (or systems) of thought (or thoughts) has barely been reported in the popular media; publishers, editors and broadcasting executives would argue, no doubt, that the public doesn't really care one way or the other. The populist/pragmatist Richard Rorty, a professional philosopher, has gained a bit of coverage and notoriety for speaking publicly of Philosophy's demise. But his reports from the front are, in my opinion, often too technical and often too simplistic — and often both at once. Moreover, given his position as a distinguished member of the Philosophy Department at the University of Virginia, Rorty's *reportage* is somewhat suspect; after all, even without analytical training most ordinary people are suspicious when someone stands up to announce: "I am dead."

As with the death of any full-blown system of knowledge, the end of Philosophy presents us with the task of answering one by one the hard questions that used to be taken care of by the departed system. What is needed, in my view, is a new method: a new, *non-systematic* way of answering the still relevant questions once covered by the philosophical system. Wittgenstein's work is invaluable in this enterprise. For he was not only Philosophy's attending physician in its last days, but also the discoverer of a marvelous method — the method of the language game, or philosophizing without Philosophy — for going forward.

Both the death of Philosophy and the birth of Wittgenstein's method have, in my view, profound implications for other systematic disciplines — most especially Philosophy's 100-year-old child, Psychology. For Wittgenstein's philosophizing without Philosophy has not simply helped to put Philosophy out of its misery. It has generated, first, a small army of philosophers called "philosophical psychologists" and, more recently and more importantly, a growing number of psychologists who are skillful at philosophizing. Kenneth Gergen (the author of *The Saturated Self*), an important member of this latter grouping, has influenced me the most in recent years.

A founding father of the "psychological philosophers" (although so far as anyone knows he never heard of Wittgenstein) was the early Soviet psychologist Lev Vygotsky (1896-1934). Suppressed under Stalin, Vygotsky's foundational works in psychology and culture were largely unavailable in

English and other languages until the 1970s and '80s. Today, however, Wittgenstein and Vygotsky, in tandem, are busy burying Psychology — dead or alive. As with the death of Philosophy, Psychology's demise-in-process demands a new, non-systematic method to answer the still relevant questions that it used to take care of: questions about human life in general, and the life of the mind in particular.

But why, you may wonder, *must the method we seek be non-systematic?* Here we come to still another postmodern implication of the death of Philosophy (and, in turn, of Psychology). For as Wittgenstein (followed by many others) teaches us, the terminal illness of parent and child is inseparable from the overall failure of systemization itself in this, the 20th century (manifested in everything from the collapse of the effort to systemize the foundations of Mathematics and Logic to the Soviet-Stalinist destruction of international Communism). Thus it is that Science, the paradigmatic embodiment of systemization in modernist culture, is itself under devastating assault by Wittgenstein, Vygotsky, and their critical theoretic pals...yours truly included.

Performance of a Lifetime is a product of some 35 years of work inside, outside, but most importantly independent of, the university system — a system that, in my opinion, overdetermines all creative thinking and most particularly all creative thinking about systems (including anti-systems). The book itself (this introduction notwithstanding) is, I hope, accessible and of use to ordinary people who seek to live more developmentally and more joyously. But having written it (with the help of the dear friend and colleague of mine you just met in the Preface, Dr. Phyllis Goldberg, a sociologist who does philosophizing very well indeed), I felt a strong need to give you, the reader, one insider's view of the astounding and as yet almost unheard of revolution against systemization that is now under way. The mass media, in certain respects like our society itself, have been so preoccupied with Socialism and Communism — revolution(s) that failed — that they've barely covered the revolution which is succeeding. I believe that the postmodern revolt against systems and Modernism (as a system of systems) is what will shape human life in the 21st century.

Certainly you can read *Performance of a Lifetime* without its overly technical introduction. Arguably, it would be better that way. But that's for you to decide, not me. You might find it interesting to read the introduction again after you've finished the rest of the book (which is the way I wrote it) to see how — or whether — my current understanding and/or practice of philosophizing informs your understanding of Philosophy in its death throes. In any event, please forgive my modest discussions of and about technical Philosophy. Think of this introduction as an obituary written by the child of a dead parent.

I first studied Philosophy formally in the summer of 1956 at the City College of New York. I had just returned to college after almost three years in the U.S. Army, including 16 months in Korea. It was my good fortune to wind up, purely by chance, in an Introduction to Philosophy course taught by a professor named K.D. Irani. An exceedingly erudite Parsee Indian (if I remember correctly) and, as I came to discover, a minor cult figure among City College undergraduates, Irani talked...philosophically. Somehow I connected to his way of speaking, even as I learned little or nothing about Philosophy. He and I spoke to each other often in class and I became kind of a "follower." But my papers and tests (when I wrote or took them) revealed that I knew nothing of Philosophy. Irani, quite properly, although somewhat reluctantly, gave me an "F" in the course. So began my career in Philosophy; I have been a failure at it for almost 40 years now. Between 1956 and 1959 I took enough courses in Philosophy (many with Irani, and a few that I passed) to graduate (barely) from CCNY as a Philosophy major.

I am the youngest of five children from a lower working class Jewish family in the southwest Bronx. Like my parents, my older brothers and my sister hadn't finished high school, still less gone on to college. As a teenager I worked part-time as a stock clerk, a salesman, and a machine shop assistant; when I graduated from Stuyvesant High School in 1952 I had no serious plans to continue my education. (In my high school yearbook I said that I hoped to go to the University of Alabama, but I made that up because the sportscaster for the New York Yankees at the time, Mel Allen, had gone there.) After high school I got a job in a leather goods shop on West 32nd Street in Manhattan. College, let alone Philosophy, was not on my agenda.

A friend of mine, Dave, with whom I went straight through public school, junior high school, and high school, had entered CCNY in the fall of 1952, and when we got together once a week or so he'd encourage me to "take the test for City." I hated the leather goods job about as much as I hated sales and the machine shop, so eventually I did. I passed the test, got admitted, and in February of '53 found myself on the Harlem campus of CCNY knowing nothing of colleges and universities — except for their sports teams. (I did know one other thing, which was that CCNY had no tuition. That, unfortunately, has since changed.)

In the two years before I got there, City College had gone from boasting one of the greatest college basketball teams in history — the only team (to this day) ever to have won both the National Collegiate Athletic Association (NCAA) tournament and the National Invitational Tournament (NIT) in the same season — to being scandalized by the revelation that during their champion season many of the team's top players — mainly Black and Jewish working class kids — had taken money (not very much, as it turned out) from gamblers to fix games by "shaving" points. (Imagine how good they might have been if they had played their best!)

Academically speaking, my freshman year was a continuation of my deplorable high school career, which, in turn, had been a continuation of my dreadful junior high school career, which, in turn, was completely consistent with my awful academic work in the fifth and sixth grades. I had not been any kind of a student at all since 1945, when my father died suddenly (at a relatively young age) just before I turned 10. I did fall madly in love in the spring of that freshman year with a young woman named Flo. But when it became apparent that this beautiful and wonderful relationship was also (under the serious pressure of outside influences) going to fail, I joined the Army to make things easier for both Flo and me.

Now, three years later, in the summer of 1956, I had come back to City College, older and more worldly-wise than most of the other students — and still profoundly unsure about what I was doing with my life and, more specifically, what in the hell I was doing in college. If I remember correctly, it was a very humid summer. I sat in Professor Irani's classroom in old Wagner Hall on the City College south campus, at 21 an emotionally devastated failure, enjoying very little of life except — sometimes — when I was listening to Irani talk philosophically.

Time passed, as it tends to do, and by the spring of 1959 I was close to completing my BA in Philosophy at CCNY, married (not, of course, to Flo), and trying to figure out what to do with a degree in Philosophy (not to mention a completely undistinguished undergraduate career in it...and everything else, for that matter). What emerged as the guiding principle in my scattered and less than rational deliberations was: "Get as far away from New York City — that is, your failures and unhappiness — as possible." Accordingly, I applied to Stanford University, a truly first-rate school (at the time, I didn't even know that), because it was far away in Palo Alto, California.

I applied to Stanford almost a month after the closing date for admission applications and, remarkably, was accepted. I later found out that someone who had previously accepted an offer from the Graduate School changed her or his mind and went, instead, to Harvard, thereby creating an opening. Since my belated application was the only "live" one Stanford had (and, at that point, was likely to get), I got in despite my awful record. Friends told me afterward that members of the Philosophy faculty at Stanford had been somewhat intrigued by the letters of recommendation they got from several of my CCNY Philosophy teachers, who all said things like, "Don't be put off by his unbelievably lousy record...he's actually kind of bright." Anyway, "miracle of miracles," I entered Stanford University as a Ph.D. candidate in Philosophy.

Barbara, the woman I was married to at the time, had a job as a social worker. I had one year left of my G.I. Bill money. So I didn't have to work that academic year, 1959-60. The learning environment at Stanford was extraordinary (good teachers, small classes, beautiful weather, gorgeous campus, wonderful friends, and fellow graduate students...). And so, despite a traumatic (although ultimately successful) year-long struggle with symbolic logic, I made the great academic comeback. In the spring of my second year I easily passed my comprehensive exams and consequently received enough scholarship and teaching assistant money to continue my Ph.D. studies.

When I got to Stanford I had some vague idea of studying Oriental philosophy. (I had taken a couple of history courses with Arthur Tiedemann, a distinguished Asian Studies scholar at CCNY.) But as I soon realized, the "happening" philosophical topics at Stanford in those years were the philosophy of mind (philosophical psychology), the philosophy of language, logic, and the philosophy of science. The "happening" philosopher was Donald Davidson, who, some 35 years later, and now in his mid-seventies, is one of the world's most distinguished professional philosophers. Starting in my second year, I took several courses with Donald. I also attended some of the by-invitation-only informal seminars he conducted at his stunningly beautiful house in the hills overlooking the campus. Together we studied the latest work of Philosophers like Strawson *(Individuals),* Hampshire *(Thought and Action),* J.L. Austin *(Sense and Sensibilia),* Quine *(Word and Object),* Chomsky *(Syntactic Structures),* and many others. Davidson, a notorious non-publisher of books and articles in his younger days, was considering and developing the themes that ultimately came together in his seminal paper "Actions, Reasons and Causes." (It was originally presented in a symposium on "Action" at the 1963 meetings of the American Philosophical Association.)

Davidson was a brilliant teacher with an absolutely first-rate mind. He was already known in the field as a formidable philosopher (even before he began publishing regularly). Also "present" (although not physically) was Ludwig Wittgenstein, who had died in '51 and whose work (including *Philosophical Inves-*

tigations), along with the writings of the first wave of his post-humous followers, was just becoming available in the late '50s. Dan Bennett, a young faculty member and a recent Stanford Ph.D., a friend and a mentor to me, was, at least as I saw it, the resident Wittgensteinian. Both Dan and Wittgenstein were anywhere from a little to a lot over my head; much of what they had to teach me only became apparent many years later. Davidson was not, it seemed to me, a Wittgensteinian — although what he was, other than a philosophical genius (and a good tennis doubles partner) was less clear. Certainly, you could make out the empiricistic, neo-positivistic, Tarskian (Tarski thought little of Wittgenstein), Hempelian, Quinian, decision-theoretic (Davidson and Patrick Suppes, his colleague at Stanford, had written a book together on decision theory) influences on his thinking. In some ways, it seemed to me, Davidson was trying to construct a theory of action and reason which was structurally analogous to Tarski's correspondence theory of truth (often summed up as follows: The sentence "It is snowing" is true if and only if it is snowing).

What Davidson eventually arrived at (so far as I've been able to tell, then and now) was the very interesting position (following, among others, his former colleague, the distinguished positivist philosopher of science Carl Hempel, who was then at Princeton University) that explanations or accountings of *human actions* given in terms of *reasons* are both causally and structurally the same as, or very similar to, explanations of events (especially non-human events) in the so-called hard or natural sciences. That is, the model of explanation operative (or at least said to be by methodologists and philosophers of science) in the hard sciences — sometimes called a "causal" or a "deductive-nomological" model — suffices, in the form of reasons, for the softer social sciences and/or ordinary, conversational accountings of human actions. In other words, while reasons may not be the same thing as causes, they play the same role in explaining human actions as causes do in explaining physical events. Back then (this was the late '50s), many philosophers of mind/philosophical psychologists — including those who had been strongly influenced by Wittgenstein (particularly his later writings) — were beginning to attack this neo-positivist, deductive-nomological thesis.

Point of history: By then, Logical Positivism had essentially been destroyed as a philosophical "school." In his remarkable essay "Two Dogmas of Empiricism" (an early version was first presented in 1950), Harvard's W.V.O. Quine assumed leadership of the pack that had, with devastating accuracy, been taking critical aim at Positivism, the most sophisticated expression of British Empiricism in the 20th century, and its spokespersons in the Vienna Circle. Quine's subsequent effort (in *Word and Object*, 1963) to resurrect Empiricism, via C.I. Lewis-style epistemological Pragmatism, without the dogmas (the dogma of reductionism and the dogma of the analytic-synthetic distinction) had been privately dubbed by Davidson — who greatly respected Quine — "the last gasp of Empiricism." Apparently, Davidson (following Frege, Tarski and others) saw himself as having analytically leaped beyond Humean Empiricism to a kind of Analyticism which, of course, was more than consistent with empirics but which broke completely with the metaphysics of Empiricism. Indeed, in my opinion, he succeeded in doing so. Ultimately, however, Davidson himself became one of *Philosophy's* most significant "last gasps."

Forgive all this philosophical name and idea dropping. But the fact is that something of considerable importance was going on, although I did not see it very clearly then and therefore did not participate in it very actively or self-consciously for some time to come. Under the ever-emerging influence of Ludwig Wittgenstein, Philosophy was being challenged. At the same time, the philosophical roots of postmodern deconstructionism were beginning to take hold; three decades later, in the 1980s and '90s, they would become the basis for a serious challenge to Psychology and, in turn, for a challenge to Science itself.

Certainly critical scholars in various parts of the European academic world (Habermas, Foucault, Derrida and others), who were raising different issues in different ways, can also lay claim to igniting the postmodern revolt against modern science (and the 300-year-old absolute authority of the scientific paradigm). But America had by then become the home away from home of European Psychology, Modernism and science. The Wittgensteinian revolution (which, as we approach the 21st century, is turning out to be vastly more important than either the Marxian or the Freudian one) was, from the late '50s through the '60s and '70s, quietly germinating within the American university system. Its history over these last 35 years inside that system and, at least as importantly (I would argue, no doubt self-servingly), outside the system must be understood if we are (these days) to understand understanding (and, therefore, anything) at all.

Most everyone in Stanford's graduate Philosophy program in the early '60s was a Davidsonian. I quickly became interested, under the mentorship of Professor David Nivison, in the topic of historical explanation. Hempel had written an important essay called "The Function of General Laws in History," in which he claimed that while general laws and empirical observation were typically less evolved in the "science" of history than in science in general, the characteristic unstated explanatory model of history (writing and research) was roughly the same as in physics, biology, and chemistry. Later on, Davidson would acknowledge his debt to Hempel (in "Hempel on Explaining Action," which was read at a celebration in honor of Hempel at Princeton University in November of 1975), although during the years when I was at Stanford ('59-'62) he hardly ever referred to Hempel's work. In any event, Hempel's seminal essay (which by then appeared in various anthologies) was a turning point in the emergence of 20th century philosophy of history. (Pre-20th century philosophy of history, from Vico through Hegel and Dilthey to Collingwood, had a somewhat dishonorable past — at least in the eyes of analytic philosophers.)

My early thinking about "explanation in history" was completely Hempelian and, of course, Davidsonian. At this time a number of new Wittgenstein-influenced books on the subject had begun to appear. Perhaps one of the most important was *Laws and Explanation in History*, by the Canadian philosopher William Dray. Obviously influenced by so-called "ordinary language" and "ordinary language philosophy" (said to derive, by way of J.L. Austin, from Wittgenstein's later work), Dray argued that not all explanations, and especially not all historical explanations, are causal answers to *why* questions at all; accounting for something in history often merely involves saying, in some detail, *what* happened or *how* it happened or, indeed, simply *how it was possible* that it happened. None of these, Dray said, required causal-deductive underpinnings. And neither did all historical explanations.

Michael Scriven, a philosopher of science at Indiana University, backed Dray up (or vice versa) by insisting that

Hempel confused a historical explanation with the grounds which might justify either the explanation itself or the *giving* of the explanation. And so on. And so on. Numerous young and not so young philosophers began to write about the philosophy of history in general and historical explanation in particular. My first writings on the subject, which included my doctoral dissertation, were Hempelian and Davidsonian. But sometime during my third and last year at Stanford (perhaps my friend Dan Bennett's Wittgensteinianism was sinking in), it occurred to me that maybe the critiques of Hempel by Dray, Scriven and others were not utterly trivial.

What had always put me off about the anti-Hempelians' insistence that the context in which the explanation was given was a critical factor in the analysis of the explanation itself was that including or excluding the context confused the critical distinction between what an *explanation* was and what the *activity of explaining* was. But what if there was no distinction? What if the philosophical-explicative *activity* (for example, the explication or "unfolding" of explanation) ultimately could not yield an abstract *explicandum*...that is, what if it could not yield some kind of philosophical definition? What if it could only yield itself as activity? What if (following the later Wittgenstein) the entire philosophical activity could not yield Philosophical Truths but merely more and more activity? Yet weren't Dray and Scriven also suggesting (or at least implying) that context could somehow be explicated philosophically? That is, wasn't their context just as troublesome as Hempel's explanation? For didn't the analysis of context fail to take into account the context in which context was itself analyzed? And wasn't activity itself just another word or concept? And so on. This was 20 years before I was introduced to Lev Vygotsky and *activity theory* and, more importantly, 10 years before I discovered, in theory and practice, that practical/critical activity as understood by Karl Marx is an activity — not words.

Sometime late in that third and final year of graduate school, in a formal seminar with Davidson, I made my first, utterly naive, effort to talk about activity as extra-linguistic. It was a total debacle. Davidson and his analytical "gang" of graduate students and young professors tore into me with a vengeance. The essence of their critique, as far as I could tell, was that the study of the activity of "doing philosophy" was not itself a proper subject for Philosophy. Maybe it was worthy of consideration by someone interested in the "sociology of knowledge," but it was not Philosophy. Here is their argument: You may, a la Dray and Scriven, distinguish between what a proper *explication* of explanation is (philosophically speaking) and what the *activity* of explaining is (philosophically speaking) — although it is (philosophically speaking) a mistake to do so. But if you seek to include the activity of doing philosophy as relevant to what you discover by participating in that activity, you haven't simply made a philosophical error. You've committed what Gilbert Ryle, the British philosopher of mind, smugly called "a category mistake": mixing apples and oranges, leaving yourself open to a kind of self-referential paradox, abandoning Philosophy as a discernible, boundaried field of study. In a word (or rather two words), you were making a damned fool of yourself. After almost three years of success, I had failed Philosophy once again.

From my earliest moments with Irani, I had felt closer to the activity of doing philosophy than to Philosophy. Now it was six years later and I was about to receive my official certification (a Ph.D.) as a philosopher. But I had no idea what, or whether, it — Philosophy — was. And yet only a year earlier I had been thinking that I did! Moreover, I was about to start getting paychecks for knowing what Philosophy was.

In the fall of 1962 I set out for Galesburg, Illinois. This is the home of Knox College, an undergraduate liberal arts school, where I had been hired to teach Philosophy — whatever the hell it was. Not knowing what it was did not stand in the way of "talking philosophically" — the activity of philosophy — and very quickly I became a most popular and, I believe, skillful teacher (I had extraordinary models in Irani and Davidson). Indeed, the two (not knowing what Philosophy was and philosophizing) were connected. Feeling no obligation to "prop up" Philosophy helped me to bring the method of philosophy (although not yet Wittgensteinian language games) into many different modes of discourse. During the three years between 1962 and 1965 I spent at Knox, I played an important role in developing cross-disciplinary programs (formal and informal). I also became very active in campus community life. Much to the administration's dismay, I brought the philosophical method out of the classroom and into the world of Knox. I first began to see (although dimly) how philosophizing could help build community beyond the hundred or so students formally taking courses for credit with me.

I returned to CCNY as a full-fledged faculty member in the fall of 1965. The civil rights movement and the anti-Vietnam War movement were already percolating at City College, even as what has become known as "the Sixties" was emerging nationally. In this environment my love/hate relationship with philosophizing/Philosophy blossomed, and I more self-consciously transformed my classes into communities. As you

might imagine, the college administration was not thrilled —
least of all when I took what they saw as an extreme step (to
me it was simply consistent with a communitarian approach to
philosophizing) by giving all of my students A's.

I saw this decision as an anti-war protest as well, since
men students' eligibility for the draft was largely determined
by their grade point average — the lower your grades, the
more likely you were to be drafted. I gave my women students
A's also since it would have been discriminatory and sexist to
exempt them; they were as much a part of the community as
men. Moreover, it was becoming increasingly apparent to me
that while it might make sense to grade students on how much
Philosophy they *knew*, it made no sense to grade them on how
well they *did* philosophizing — that is, *participated in the learning community*. Over the next two years (between '66 and '68)
I practiced this philosophical communitarian method at several schools across the country — without ever finding, you
will not be surprised to hear, a single college or university
administration that liked it at all. In their view, I was failing
Philosophy — that is, not honoring my contract. (They were
right, of course.)

By 1968 I had begun to re-examine my attitude toward
the anti-war movement and the civil rights movement. (My
moral objections to the war and to racial bigotry were intact,
but I had political objections to how the movements were
organized.) Moreover, I had come to believe that setting up
philosophizing communities within the structure of the university was an act of intellectual, moral and political dishonesty
on my part. For it had occurred to me that *the point of it all*
was not simply to negate existing structures, systems or ideas
(Philosophy, the University, Bigotry, whatever) but to build
something: an environment, a community free of the assump-

tions of these systems and, indeed, free not of *all* assumptions (I did not and still do not believe that possible) but free of the assumption that all building (or activity) necessarily involves systemization.

So in the spring and summer of 1968 (while a few other things, such as the assassination first of Dr. King and then of Robert Kennedy, were going on), I set out with a handful of students and support from an even smaller handful of faculty members (mainly from CCNY) to build (to try to build) an unstructured (unsystemized) learning/development community environment — an overwhelmingly complicated and apparently impossible task.

It is now almost 30 years later. The Sixties (along with Philosophy) is long dead and buried — although in both cases the after-image lingers on. The thousands of alternative schools (including the so-called "free" universities) that sprang up in the late '60s and early '70s are gone. Most lasted less than a year — many just a week. Our community — which includes tens of thousands of people all over America and the world, and which has produced (among many other things) this book — continues to grow quantitatively and, even more importantly, qualitatively. While we now have a collective *developmental* understanding beyond what any of us could ever have imagined in 1968, we remain unsystemized. We have gained anywhere from modest to significant international recognition for our discoveries in what are traditionally called Psychology, Pedagogy, Politics, and Culture, but we remain unsystemized. A few people have even come to study us in an effort — often, although not always, with the best of intentions — to systemize us. We remain unsystemized. Yet the fact of our continued existence means, in my opinion, absolutely nothing unless we are creating and/or discovering something of value to everyone. For Utopias, after all, are simply other self-serving systems.

From the very beginning we decided neither to ask for nor to accept major financial support, public or private, but to depend upon our own communitarian skills and energies to raise our own dollars and, thereby, to support the maintenance and growth of the community. Large donations, whether public or private, we reasoned, bring with them not merely assumptions held by the donor but a more overriding assumption that our work must be, in the final analysis, systematic — that is, that it must be understandable in terms of the models or paradigms of Science and Reason as opposed to life (practical-critical) activity and development.

Indeed, it is only in the past five years or so that we have learned to communicate our work to a broader audience without systemizing it in ways that are transparently distortive. The book you are reading is one of many successful efforts to do so. What I am asking is not that you, the reader, understand something *about* our work and *about* our community, but that you participate in it to whatever extent and in whatever ways you choose (including, of course, not at all). I have tried to create this book in such a way as to reveal the activity (the process) of its creation. Have I done so? I am in no position, and *have no need*, to judge.

One of our community's first developmental/learning activities back in 1969 was to study symbolic logic at the same time (in the same place) as we examined the "mental blocks" to learning symbolic logic, a notoriously difficult subject matter for many people. The developmental/learning activity was jointly led by a trained logician (me) and a trained psychotherapist (a psychologist or social worker), with neither "subject" (logic or psychology) being set up as dominant. Some "classes" began with logic and stayed there. Others began with problems of learning and stayed there. Many, the most difficult to begin with, went back and forth distractingly. For example, in the midst of considering the truth-table definition of the conditional (p É q) — if p, then q — someone would raise "a point of psychology": "Why don't I get it?" or "Why don't I want to get it?" The psychologist/social worker might ask: "Why *don't* you want to get it?" Then, disturbingly, someone else would say: "Why do logicians say '(p É q)' is true when both 'p' and 'q' are false?" *Now* what did we do? Some of those in the room wanted to do logic; some psychology; some neither; some both. Many didn't know what they wanted to do; some didn't see the relevance of wanting or not wanting; and so on.

A year or so later I became involved in an intense day-long debate with an old friend from Stanford, John Wallace, a very bright logician who was then teaching at Princeton. The debate, which took place at one of our community's apartment/centers, was about whether or not the context — primarily the subjective context — in which logic was done or taught or whatever was relevant to the logic. Not surprisingly, John insisted that the psychological context didn't matter. Just as unsurprisingly, I disagreed. Somewhat surprisingly, the debate rapidly transformed into a heated discussion not about logic or psychology but about morality and politics. Eventually, we at least reached the conclusion that the procedure for deciding who was right in our debate about logic and psychology would likely be determined by where we were. That is, I'd probably "win" in the community apartment; he'd most likely "win" at Princeton.

Far more important than who won or lost, or the specifics of this particular debate, over the ensuing months and years we as a community would become more experienced and more skilled in creating the psychological environment necessary for learning/development to take place. And in doing so we would come to see more clearly what this unsystematic mode/activity of developmental learning was.

Therapy was always important in our emerging learning community, even if we didn't quite know or agree on what it was. But many people in the community (although by no means all) wanted or asked for, or were sometimes thought by other people to need, help with their "emotional problems." Almost from the outset the therapy was seen as something not set aside and separate from community life but continuous with it. The evolution of an unsystematic clinical approach using elements of every and any existing psychology (and whatever else) was on the agenda from the beginning. "Social therapy" emerged by the late '70s as the name we gave to this unusual practice, which (paraphrasing Vygotsky) I call "creating our own clinical psychology."

Philosophy (more precisely, philosophizing) was, of course, with us from the start. However, we did not discover Wittgenstein (or, in my case, rediscover him) until sometime in the early '80s. This was after Dr. Lois Holzman, now my chief intellectual collaborator, brought Lev Vygotsky to us; she had been introduced to Vygotsky while doing groundbreaking work on "ecological validity" (the role of context in the laboratory/learning situation) at Michael Cole's Laboratory for Comparative Human Cognition, which was then located at Rockefeller University in New York City.

By the latter part of the 1980s Wittgenstein and Vygotsky were collaborating within the clinical and pedagogical environments of what was now our rapidly expanding community. For many years, *the idea of development* had languished within the confines of academic Psychology as a fundamentally cognitive, value-laden conception (having to do with the achievement of "goals"). As such it had virtually no scientific importance, and was dying a slow death. Introduced into the clinical environment of our social therapeutic practice, *development* came back to life. By the '90s, the Wittgenstein-Vygotsky collaboration had borne sufficient fruit for Routledge, the British publishing house, to invite Lois and me to co-author a book on Vygotsky for its distinguished Critical Psychology series. Our *Lev Vygotsky: Revolutionary Scientist*, which came out in 1993, was a work report from the Vygotskian "zone of proximal development" which she and I, along with many other people, had been working to build for more than 20 years: a community of non-philosophers who, under the growing influence of Ludwig Wittgenstein, were engaged in the day to day, practical-critical activity of philosophizing without Philosophy.

Politics, in the broad Aristotelian sense that it is the study of how groups of people relate to other groups of people, was also always present (as it was, unfortunately, in many narrower, more sectarian senses of the word). Nevertheless, our effort to create something positive — not merely to engage in negative polemics — dominated our unsystematic (although, I hope, never unprincipled) politics.

How do we find ways for varied and disparate groupings to create something positive together? Even in our earliest days we were already questioning the then dominant liberal paradigm of what has come to be called identity politics. From our beginnings we have been engaged in an evolving effort to create what Kenneth Gergen calls *relational* politics. That is, we were building not merely coalitions but politics sensitive to the social fact that, whatever people seek to do politically, whether as individuals or as an identified group, they must acknowledge the relational Others. Because in the most fundamental sense *we are the Others!*

Performing came a little later (the middle of the '80s) to our community, but it quickly became central to our theory and practice. Vygotsky's concern with play and Wittgenstein's language games "completed" (in Vygotsky's sense) each other and were joined with our recognition that Culture overdetermines how people *see* even as Psychology overdetermines how we *feel* and Reason overdetermines how we *think*.

Enough! You have a book to read...if you choose to. Our community lives and breathes and grows unsystematically, even as human life does. Welcome to *Performance of a Lifetime*.

I

PHILOSOPHIZING
WITHOUT
PHILOSOPHY

You're at the supermarket trying to figure out whether to make chicken or hamburgers for dinner this evening. Or you're frustrated to discover that the computers are down at work. Perhaps you're standing on a cold street corner wishing you could recall if the No. 2 bus still stops at 34th Street, because if it doesn't you'll have to go all the way up to 72nd Street and then come back down. These quite specific, concrete, unremarkable moments of everyday life and a trillion others like them hardly seem the time for philosophizing. Yet it is precisely when we're immersed in such mundane societal moments, in my opinion, that ordinary people most need to philosophize (and thereby to see our historicalness) if we are to live joyously.

It's in those very moments when we're most caught up in the immediately pressing, practical questions of everyday life — how much the groceries cost, whether a piece of work can get done by the end of the day, what the fastest way is to travel uptown — that we need to recognize ourselves as the makers not only of hamburgers, deadlines, and dates but also of the ongoing, creative social and cultural process that is history, which is the totality of what there is...at least here on Earth!

Now wait just a minute, Fred! I can almost hear you objecting. *Didn't you say a few pages ago that Philosophy is dead, or at least dying? I don't know any Philosophy, thank you, and I don't think I care to learn. As for History...I had to learn some of that, and frankly I found it pretty boring. You're telling me I have to know History to live a joyous life?*

Not at all. It makes sense to me that you're not eager to be introduced to a (dead) body of knowledge, not to mention all those dead philosophers — or to memorize the Gettysburg Address again. I want to show you how to do a very different kind of learning — learning that's not deadly, but developmental. The point isn't to know History (the "subject"), but to see yourself as a maker/performer of history (the collective life that human beings create together out of what there is). I'm here to direct you in a performance of philosophizing — the *Performance of a Lifetime* — an activity which opens the door to living joyously.

Joyousness, in my view, is to be found in our ability to experience in an ongoing way the very practical human paradox which is the knotty *intertwining* of our banality and our grandness — in living with the ever-present recognition of how little we are and of how big we are. Without that experience, we cannot know ourselves (either as individuals or as a species) fully; we remain painfully, often miserably, estranged from ourselves and, of course, those critical relational others.

The choice between chicken and hamburgers is at once of real societal significance and of no historical importance whatsoever. Maybe the five-year-old in your family refuses to eat anything except hamburger, while the grownups would occasionally like to eat something that they regard as slightly more interesting. Such things matter, sometimes intensely, to everyone involved. And yet the totality of the life (the history) that these few people, together with the rest of our species, are creating together isn't reducible to, or defined by, any of the particular things they eat, say, feel, think or do at any particular moment.

I believe that the joy of life most manifests itself in the recognition that hamburgers, and hamburger-eating, are at once both societally significant *and* historically trivial. It seems to me that most religions, in one way or another, acknowledge this paradox; "Man does not live by bread alone" is one of many statements that give expression to it. At the same time a religious outlook is typically concerned with human beings as the creatures of a supreme being, above history, and not with human beings as the creators of history. Yet most people in the world these days would agree that we are both.

Philosophizing is an activity that allows us to experience our historicalness. In the absence of philosophizing, most of us tend to see ourselves as products of the societal here-and-now who are entirely determined by the particular circumstances of our individual and individuated lives. We typically aren't aware of ourselves as the producers, along with every other human being (past, present, and future), of the cultural-historical totality of our species' life. In other words, in the absence of philosophizing it's exceedingly difficult for us to know who we are historically; lacking a sense of history we're unable to discover ourselves in that juncture (*culture*, in the broadest sense) where history and society meet — which is where I think joyousness lies.

Stop that philosophizing! they say

Yet philosophizing is more and more being rooted out from

the life activity of ordinary people. Indeed, whenever ordinary people do presume to think independently and philosophically (which more and more Americans have been trying to do in the most recent years) the powers-that-be come down on them very hard. To philosophize, to think unusual, developmental thoughts — which is what I mean by thinking — if you are not one of the officially sanctioned "geniuses," or at least "authorities," is potentially dangerous in contemporary society, regardless of *what* your thinking is. (Witness the brutal attacks, sometimes carried out directly by government agencies, on so-called "cults.")

It has not always been this way. While philosophizing has long been dangerous in Western culture — people with diverse philosophies were burned at the stake for it in earlier centuries, and in more recent times those labeled political "heretics" have been punished harshly — the subtle and pervasive demand for conformity now dominates it completely. Americans spend more hours a day watching television than they do anything else except working and sleeping. Mass education induces nearly as much passivity as mass communication. Between them, the mass media and the public education system (as well as its private counterparts) have systematically — if not conspiratorially — succeeded in rendering philosophizing an endangered species activity.

This critical fact of postmodern life has engendered enormous moral, social, and political problems. The problems get written and talked about endlessly — unfortunately, mostly by the officially sanctioned (and salaried) professional thinkers, and most frequently to each other.

But the *psychological* consequences of the "dumbing down" of America are not often considered — and when they are, the official thinkers prove conclusively, in my opinion, that they're the ones who've been dumbed down most of all. Every now and then, for example, we hear that a committee of experts — sometimes they're conservatives, sometimes they're liberals — is being established to conduct "research" into the psychological impact of *showing* violence to young children on TV. Three years later they publish their findings, and a foolish debate ensues over their conclusions. Then it's all over until the next committee is created. Yet I don't know of any government agency, or private foundation or think tank, which has attempted to investigate the impact on all of us of the violence that *is* contemporary society!

In conditioning us not to think unusually and developmentally, the mass media and mass education are making joyousness less and less possible to achieve. For it is only our capacity to philosophize that allows us to glimpse our historicalness even as we go about the business of our day to day societal lives: making meals, doing our jobs, catching the right bus.

In the absence of philosophizing, history has become yet another commodity; it's identified with, and trivialized as, the frequently tedious assignments youngsters have to do in exchange for a grade, and with whatever appeared on the 6 o'clock news. (If you missed it — History — you can always catch it again at 11 p.m.) Our capacity for philosophizing, an activity that is necessary if we are to experience our historicalness, has been terribly and tyrannically diminished — and with it our capacity for living joyously. Ironically, the extraordinarily advanced technology now available to us, which could be a source of unlimited progress (and, with it, joyousness, for billions of people), has been institutionally shaped so as to endanger the continued psychological and moral development of our species altogether. It's particularly ironic that this technology has accompanied the ascendance of modern science, which is a product of the Western philosophical tradition of dualism that originated in ancient Greece some 2,500 years ago. (I'll say more about dualism later on.)

Big questions about little things

Not surprisingly, when most people in our culture think about philosophizing (if they think about it at all) they tend to identify it with Philosophy — an exclusive, institutionalized academic "thing" that only a handful of professional thinkers are sufficiently qualified and privileged to think about. The content of this thing is what the great, usually dead, philosophers had to say about Truth, Beauty, Reality, Good and Evil, and the few other subjects considered appropriate for Philosophical inquiry. However, thinking about something that Socrates said is not at all the same as philosophizing — any more than thinking about something Michael Jordan did is the same as playing basketball.

Philosophizing is a fundamentally social activity; the characteristic form that it takes is a dialogue. It's not any old sort of conversation, although it may be about any old thing. Philosophical dialogue consists largely of asking questions and clarifying what we mean by them. More precisely, it consists of asking "big" questions about "little" things…which is one reason that people (including therapists) who do it can sometimes seem a little odd: *What does she mean by asking me what I mean when I say that I'm angry?*

Another reason, of course, is that it's not something most ordinary people do, having been denied access to the terms and techniques that make philosophizing possible — and then told that we're not qualified to engage in it.

Here, then, is a dilemma. If we are to live joyously, it seems to me, we must be able to appreciate our historicalness

— which requires that we engage in philosophical activity. But ordinary people are not in the habit of philosophizing. They may not be especially inclined to philosophize. They don't know how to do it. Does that mean that most people in our culture must resign themselves to living joylessly? I don't think so. I think we can perform our way out of this dilemma in the same way that very young children perform their way out of *their* "dilemma": They're not in the habit of speaking; they haven't been around long enough. They don't "want" to speak; why should they? They don't know how to speak; how could they?

As we will see closer up in Section II, babies perform as who they aren't (that is, as speakers of the language) by creatively imitating more experienced speakers — older children and adults — who, in turn, accept the strange, babbling sounds the baby makes and talk back to him or her. The baby babbles "in response," the older children and the parents respond in turn, and then one day those peculiar noises the baby has been making begin to take shape and to be recognized as words, sentences, language! It is by participating in this profoundly social, performatory environment/joint activity that human beings learn to speak (a major developmental turning point in the life of every individual — as it was in the life of our species all those millennia ago, in that extraordinary moment when someone first said something to someone else).

Similarly, grownups can learn to philosophize. What's required is not taking courses in Philosophy in order to know which philosopher said what; that would be like enrolling new babies in English Grammar 101 at the local college in order for them to learn how to talk. Rather, it requires performing (creatively and jointly imitating) who you are not — someone who philosophizes, a participant in an ongoing social activity/environment where big questions are constantly asked about little things.

The further challenge is that the performatory dimension of everyday life, like philosophizing itself, is also denied in contemporary culture. Instead, performance — like Politics and Philosophy — is relegated to one small and very particular corner of life; it is institutionalized, professionalized, and trivialized as entertainment (*culture*, in the narrowest sense) which a few talented people produce and the rest of us passively consume.

Performing as who we aren't

While very young children are continually performing as who they aren't (although they are not yet conscious of themselves in doing so), as soon as they get even a little bit older they are told that they must "stop pretending." Instead of being supported to do what they don't know how to do, they are tested to find out what they are capable of doing and, more and more, only allowed to do that. The astounding developmental learning which is characteristic of early childhood, when young children learn in advance of their development, is replaced by the acquisition of information and rules for adding to, manipulating, and refining it — a learning that merely follows from development, and is therefore not itself developmental.

Traditional Psychology is dominated (in its practice, if not completely in its theory) by the assumption that human beings naturally stop developing after the first few years of childhood. The prevailing view is that people are born with or quickly acquire an "intelligence quotient." And, supposedly, we have some early experiences that permanently shape our personalities. While there are variations on the theme — some psychologists give more weight to genetic factors, and others emphasize the role of culture — the idea is that by the time we're five or six, or perhaps nine or ten, we have a cognitive and emotional profile, a fixed development identity, that stays with us throughout life and largely determines how much we can learn, how fast we can learn, and even the kinds of things we can learn. We may be able to go on learning, say the psychologists, but we don't continue to develop; such learning is not the catalyst for further development.

By the time we're grown up, most people in our culture have indeed stopped developing. That's not because traditional Psychology is right, but because we are rarely in environments where we are supported to perform beyond ourselves emotionally, intellectually, artistically or in any other way, except in circumstances that are in one way or another looked on as separate from everyday life: dressing up as Santa Claus; singing in the choir; stepping out onto the dance floor; playing tennis or poker or charades; participating in a fashion show for charity; taking part in a religious ceremony, such as a wedding or a funeral. No, the institution of Psychology is not right. It only appears that way, sometimes, because society is so profoundly wrong on so many educational and emotional matters.

With every institutional means at its disposal, our culture denies that history is anything other than what appears on the nightly news broadcast or in the morning headlines. Ours is a culture that strongly discourages ordinary people from philosophizing, defines performance as something that only professionals should do, and is saturated with a theory and practice of psychology which insists that for all practical purposes human development stops in early childhood. No wonder so many people in our high-tech culture find themselves living non-developmental, joyless lives.

In *Let's Develop!* I wanted to show you how to discover development in the cultural/historical activity of creating environments where people are supported to perform as who they aren't, for I believe that to develop continuously — to learn developmentally — is what it is to be human. Here I want to show you how to discover joy in the historical-cultural performance of moment to moment, day to day philosophizing. For living joyously, in my view, is what it is to live.

History and society: A necessary unity

What is it to be human? Are we simply one among many other species on the evolutionary spectrum, or are human beings a different *kind* of animal — horses of a different color, so to speak? What is our place in the universe? Who are we? What is our "nature?" Is it possible for us to change? What choices do we actually have? Can we expect to live joyfully? Or is life essentially a painful experience which at best contains occasional pleasurable moments? How are we to live? Should we do the right thing? If so, what is that? And who knows?

For thousands of years all sorts of people — philosophers, theologians, and "thinkers" of every variety — have been asking such questions, and coming up with all sorts of answers. Although ordinary people are more and more being disqualified from philosophizing by the professional thinkers among us, we humans show no signs yet of having completely lost our *capacity* for this peculiarly human activity. There are many indications that a genuine rebellion is taking place against the dumbing down of America, for example, with people of every ideological persuasion daring to challenge the assumptions that prop up the institutions of Medicine, Psychology and even Politics. (If you don't believe it, notice the harshness with which the paid thinkers and their patrons disparage, and punish, anyone who dares to suggest publicly that these institutional emperors don't have any clothes on.)

Interestingly, other living creatures appear not to have any concern whatsoever with their nature or with the rightness of how they live; they simply seem to be who they are, do what they do...and leave it at that. We speculate about them, but they — at least according to our speculations — do not come up with theories about us. We may like to think that a dog is man's best friend, but it is unlikely that Fido and Fifi (although they may even *be* our best friends) "think" of us as theirs.

Perhaps this indicates that to be invested not exclusively in physical survival, but also in the quality of life — its aesthetic and moral dimensions (the look and the value of it) — is one expression of our human-ness and of our uniqueness. This is different from saying that "the unexamined life is not worth living," which in my opinion is a fatuous, elitist, presumptuous, and platitudinous slogan. It was first uttered by one or another self-satisfied and highly privileged philosopher in ancient Greece, where more than half the population was enslaved and thereby forced by the Philosopher-Kings to live lives (examined or unexamined) characterized by desperation, deprivation and misery.

But it *is* worth noting, I think, that only human beings appear to perceive ourselves, to be consciously aware of ourselves — and almost surely it is only we who talk about ourselves — in the activity (the historical process) of living our lives.

To me, in fact, it is one of the more remarkable features of the human experience that each of us lives a life and is, simultaneously, capable of watching that life as it is being lived. That is, as human beings we participate in the making of our history *and* we're able to view ourselves, to be conscious of doing so, as we appear in our various societal circumstances and roles. If "all the world's a stage," as Shakespeare wrote, women and men are not "merely" players — we are also the audience for our own (as well as others') performances.

Sadly, more and more people in contemporary society view their lives (their performances) with little interest or compassion; more or less bored, more or less inclined to find fault, they doze or grumble their way through the "plays" in which they are the lead actors (not to mention the ones in which they have a supporting part).

Yet it is possible to learn how to look and listen with appreciation, even though what's going on may not always be wonderful, thrilling, inspiring, or even very pleasant. *Performance of a Lifetime* is about helping grownups to achieve the innocence that most people only have as little children, when we view life with a sense of wonder. It is about how to see the magic in things; to hear the music in children's laughter, old people's gossip, a neighbor's hello, a lover's whisper; to smile at the absurdity of things — including our own inclination to take ourselves, our passions, our possessions, and our opinions too seriously...or too trivially!

For I believe that one critical dimension of joy and of a joyous life is a readiness to acknowledge, accept, and appreciate your own appearance in the moment to moment-ness of everyday living — even when your life doesn't look the way you hoped it would or think it should.

Society is in many ways like a set of mirrors. Your home, your office, the movies, the mall, a PTA meeting, a friend's birthday party — the places you go because you want to be there or because you need to get something done in them — are all "looking glasses." You peer into them and see not yourself, but reflections or images of yourself. Depending on the circumstances, the mirror may show someone who's dying of cancer, the employee of the month, a jealous girlfriend, a dissatisfied customer, a proud parent, a grieving son…or any one of an infinite number of images, illusory in that they appear to *be* you when they are in fact merely *reflections* of you. This isn't to say that they're not "real." What you see when you look in the mirror are real reflections, real images, real appearances, in the same way that photographs are really what *they* are — images — but not the same as what is pictured in them.

Similarly, the constantly shifting *appearances* of your life — the illusory-though-real images you see when you look in one or another societal mirror — are very different from your historical life activity, which has to do not with how you appear but with your and everyone else's ever-evolving relationship to, with, in, as, history. If society is like a set of mirrors in which you see your self reflected in a certain light and in a particular pose, as you do in a snapshot, history is like a beginning-less and end-less improvisational (constantly emerging) play in which all of us *perform* our lives together — as individuals, in smaller ensembles such as families, friendships, and communities, and as a species; that is, socially and culturally.

It is through our continuous participation in the stabilizing institutions of society that the particularities of our individuated self-identity (our tastes, our habits, our attitudes, our opinions, and our behaviors) are determined; it is only in history that we exercise our freedom to transform the totality of life continuously. Of course, each of us is simultaneously in society *and* history. We are, accordingly, both fixed in our ways *and* free: naturally conservative in our need and ability to live institutionally stable lives — that is, to behave; and naturally revolutionary in our ongoing need and ability to change, restructure, and re-create the totality of who we are and how we live — that is, to create, to produce, to perform.

Each of us contributes — more or less, and with more or less awareness — to making history, which is at once the earthly product and the producer of everything there is. As such, of course, history includes the societal appearance of our lives as well as the mirrors themselves (which are, after all, among the things we humans make) but is other — as well as qualitatively richer — than the sum of its societal parts. History is performance. It's not another place (as in "the past"), or time (as in "19th century American History"), but a complex, performatory activity; it is the seamless, indivisible totality of our individual and species' continuous social and cultural productive performance.

It's not a matter of good or bad

The point is not that society/stability (behavior) is "bad" and history/revolutionary activity (performance) is "good," as some people seem to believe — or the other way around, as some other people tend to think. Rather, it's that as human beings we continuously create both necessary conservative societal institutions *and* equally necessary historical cultural revolution. And while there is an ongoing tension between our need for the stability provided by those societal institutions and our need to be free from the constraints they impose on us, that tension is not necessarily problematic. On the contrary, I believe that joyousness (for an individual, a family, a nation, or a world) lies in our capacity to live — and thereby to be aware that we are living — a life in which history and society continuously and conflictedly "meet."

Living joyously is, in my opinion, the uniquely human

experience of savoring the conflicted, immensely rich *relationship* between living your life (*performing*) in history and watching yourself live your life (*behaving*) in the societal mirrors. To experience that complicated and marvelous relationship requires both an activistic awareness of yourself as part of history, which neither starts nor ends with you but to which you make a unique contribution, and an appreciation of the situationally changing images of yourself that appear in the societal mirrors.

You may have that sense of joy in what seem to be, looked at from a strictly societal point of view, the most unlikely situations. Perhaps you've stopped off at the bank on the way to work to put some money into your account to cover the checks you mailed yesterday — only to find out that the automatic deposit machine isn't working. With 17 people ahead of you on the line at the teller's window, you consider your options: Take a chance that the checks will bounce and you'll have to pay the bank $60 in penalties, or arrive at work half an hour late. You're anxious, annoyed with yourself for not having made the deposit last night, irate that the bank manager isn't putting more tellers on the job...It's at that very moment, when you as your individuated self are completely caught up in these particular (and not particularly wonderful) societal circumstances, that you can allow yourself to become aware, simultaneously, of your historicalness. That is, you can come to appreciate that you are a participant along with the rest of us in the ongoing social process of creating and re-creating our world, including the extraordinary computer technology which (despite the occasional breakdown) is a quite remarkable human achievement, and a highly complex international economy which (despite being terribly mismanaged sometimes) is no less significant an accomplishment of human productivity.

It is the comprehension of ourselves as both ridiculous (we're those funny creatures who watch clocks, wait on line, maintain a balance) *and* sublime (we're the uniquely inventive species whose activity continuously transforms the totality of what there is, including ourselves) that produces joy.

Looking and looking away

Human beings are, like all other animals, biological creatures. As such, we're able to create the means of satisfying our requirements for a stable existence. And unlike any other creatures, we are (for better and for worse) self-conscious — that is, we're capable of recognizing what we produce *as* the products of our own creation.

To be aware that the societal institutions are no more than cultural artifacts which we ourselves — our species selves — make is extremely liberating; such awareness carries with it the recognition that everything can be not merely re-formed, but transformed. However, to be constantly aware of the "man-made" origins of our stability — to look unblinkingly at historical process with the naked eye of self-consciousness — can also be terrifying and terribly painful. We need to look, *and* we need to look away. The conservative societal institutions we construct are what enable us to engage in revolutionary deconstruction; the very stability of the societal institutions makes it possible for us to continue to participate in historical activity.

Alienation, our culturally fostered inclination and capacity to disregard the process of production so that all we see are its products (including self-identity), is one of the means that we have devised for protecting ourselves from being blinded by the too-brilliant constant awareness of process. But to be permanently blind *to* process is, in my opinion, at least as terrifying and painful as it is to view it relentlessly.

In my view, much of the panic and the despair which dominate the emotional experience of all too many people in contemporary culture is a consequence of the fact that we are increasingly conditioned to blind ourselves to history in this way; when our alienation is not tempered or relieved by the recognition of our historicalness, we are likely to feel trapped inside the institutionalized, behavioristic boxes constructed of societal roles and rules...with no way out.

As I see it, joyousness lies in being "at home" in our two homes, society and history. It's the experience of being in your bathtub, surrounded by what appears to be most familiar, certain and ordinary, and gazing out the window toward the unknown and perhaps unknowable grandeur of the timeless stars — all the while bathed in the beginning-lessness and end-lessness of transformable, seamless history.

Behavior and performance

In *Let's Develop!* I tried to show that as human beings we have the unique capacity to make choices about how and who we want to be. In fact, it's by continuously engaging in the activity of choosing how we live — which is, in my opinion, accomplished through creative *performance* — that people develop.

Behavior, by contrast, is the acting out of roles we've been assigned and/or have chosen to play on the basis of societal characteristics such as gender, age, ethnicity, class, and individuation in the myriad, repetitive situations of societal life. Those roles, which children begin rehearsing in the family and later on in school, contribute to the stability of the societal institutions in which we participate as adults. We appear in the societal mirrors as the Wife, the Bus Driver, the Banker, the Secretary, the Son-in-Law, the Sales Clerk, the Customer and whoever else; those roles help us to comprehend what we see there and to reassure us that we know what's going on.

Used in this way — to enable us to live our day to day lives without having to make everything up as we go along — roles and identity aren't especially problematic; ordinary life would be very complicated indeed if we all had to figure out where we were going to sleep every night, and with whom, as well as every other detail of our existence. But if the roles and rules are misused, as they typically are, to keep people "in their places," they can be terribly constraining, even crippling. When a child is told: "Behave yourself!" the speaker, unfortunately, usually means: "Obey the rules — if you don't, you'll be punished or disgraced." When a man tells himself that he's not a "real" man because he's unable to earn enough money to support his family, when a woman feels that she's not a "real" woman because she doesn't have a husband or children, they are allowing those illusory societal roles to overdetermine and dominate them — to take them over.

Similarly, behavior — which tends to be (or appear) automatic — isn't necessarily "bad." We wait our turn at the supermarket, take a shower, drop letters in the mailbox, say 'I'm sorry' if we dial the wrong number, make ourselves a sandwich, and do thousands of other things every day without having to think a whole lot about what we're doing or how we're doing them, which is often quite convenient. Yet there are times when "doing what comes naturally" (being ourselves) can be very damaging, precisely *because* we haven't stopped to think about what we're doing or how we're doing it.

Performance, by contrast, is creative. While behavior is imposed on us by the societal institutions, which require everyone to act more or less the same (even in our shared dedication to our own individuality), in performing we express our historical and social uniqueness; we are other than who we are. Interestingly, however, most people tend to identify behavior (including emotional behavior) with what is "natural" and to regard performance as "phony" — legitimate only for some few people called "actors" to do, and then only in places called "theatres." That the historical, performatory dimension of life has been so diminished, circumscribed and professionalized in our culture has everything to do, in my opinion, with the trouble most of us have in recognizing our historicalness — we are so rarely allowed to give expression to it in our everyday lives.

Yet we are a performing species! Babies, as I mentioned earlier, learn how to speak by *performing* speaking. Before they know what they're doing — before they know the role — they improvisationally imitate older children and adults, who support the little ones to go beyond themselves by doing what they don't know how to do. In this social environment, very young children don't imitate the more experienced speakers as parrots or monkeys imitate, which is simply to mimic and thereby reproduce sounds; they engage in the thoroughly social activity of creative developmental imitation, making (together with their older, societally more experienced partners) new meaning at the same time as they're learning to use the meanings that are already there. It's in *performing as who we aren't* in a social environment — with other human beings who support us to engage in that social activity — that we make the ordinary and quite miraculous leap from baby talk to the real thing.

We comes before me: The social comes first

The prevailing (orthodox) model of learning is based on the premise that individual or self-knowledge must and should come before social activity. This model is, in my opinion, profoundly misguided in that it turns the actual historical process on its head; when you look at how very young children jump from babbling to speaking (as we'll do in Section II), you see that learning actually happens the other way around. The learning I am talking about here is learning that "leads" development — not the computer-like assimilation of additional information into what someone already knows, but learning that's in advance of development and drives it forward. This learning that leads development, unlike the societal acquisition of information and the rules for adding to, using or correcting it, is thoroughly social and cultural in its origins and performatory in its character. It is only such performatory learning-leading-development, in my opinion, that enables ordinary people to philosophize, to think independently, to question assumptions, in our anti-developmental and (for all its insistence on the pleasure principle) anti-joyous culture.

The notion that children start out having some sort of impulse or instinct or imprint (perhaps even an "inner life" or sense of "self") inclining them toward speech which precedes or is a precondition for participating in the social activity of speaking — a notion that in one form or another has tended to dominate traditional thinking in psychology and psycholinguistics from the ancient Greek Plato to the thoroughly modern Chomsky — is as much a fiction, in my view, as the story of Robinson Crusoe, the original individual-unto-himself. (Even Crusoe had another human being, Friday, with whom he shared his island. And before them, Adam had Eve.)

In real — more precisely, historical — life, human beings are social before we become individuated. Babies begin by performing with (imitating) other human beings; it is only eventually that we internalize this social activity and come to have a sense of ourselves as societal individuals. It's only later on that we learn to look in the societal mirrors, where we see a self, the person we identify as "I," who thinks "my" thoughts and feels "my" feelings.

This is how all learning takes place — socially *and* individually. What I am saying here is not meant to deny or deprecate the individual dimension of learning — internalization — but to show its ongoing social basis and performatory nature. Social/historical activity is the ground from which the individual societal self emerges, not the other way around.

When a child is born, he or she immediately enters a complex set of circumstances and facts — a social activity/environment in which other people are already present, making a life (culture) together. At that moment, family life resembles a busy street that you enter simply by turning the corner. Suddenly, there you are! The hustle and bustle don't start just then; car horns were already blaring, those teenagers were already playing their radio, the police officer at the traffic circle was already yelling at the truck driver, a child was already crying, a sidewalk ice cream vendor was already calling out before you arrived — and all of it will no doubt continue after you've gone by. The other people on the street don't ask whether you know where you're going before they make room for you on the sidewalk, and you don't insist on taking lessons — in how to window shop, catch the bus, buy a newspaper, walk into a restaurant or get to the department store — before joining the crowd. It's not about knowing how, or even intending to, participate; nor does the crowd decide to make you a part of itself. You're included (even if how you're included may not be particularly respectful or caring) simply by being there, by turning the corner.

So it is with babies, who don't intend or desire to participate in the life of the family; they don't even know that they're doing so. Nor do Mommy and Daddy and the other children hold a meeting to decide whether or not to let the new baby in; families aren't clubs, with committees that review applications for membership. A new baby is included (in better or worse ways) along with everyone else in the ongoing life that everyone who's part of that household is living/creating together. Very young children only become aware of being societal individuals in the historical activity of being social.

One traditional argument for the primacy of the individual self is that human beings are born with a "predisposition" toward sociability. Perhaps we are. But whether or not we enter the world with this innate inclination (genetic or any other sort), nothing could come of it if not for the social and cultural circumstances that bring it into play.

It is one of the many fascinating contradictions of human life that while the individual self is a product of social experience, the highly complex and sophisticated process which produces it tends to erase the "memory" of how it is produced. In other words, the self can (and, increasingly in our contemporary culture, does) deny its social-historical origins; we come to believe that "I" am really, fundamentally, "naturally" the individuated self which appears in the societal mirrors, and that social life/historical performance is manufactured, artificial and imposed upon this original "me."

It is my belief that this profound misapprehension of who we are as human beings (a misunderstanding systematically reinforced by traditional, identity-based Psychology) is a principal source of the spiritual pain and isolation from which millions of people suffer in contemporary society. In their deepening alienation, they're continuously excusing themselves from the dance of history so that they can watch an "analysis" of it on the 6 o'clock news instead. Where is the remedy for such alienated pain? It lies in restoring our sense of ourselves as social-historical beings who are taking part in the ongoing creative performance that is the life activity of our species. In the absence of a sense of history, we're unable to appreciate, to enjoy, the uniquely human dialectical experience of living our lives in history/watching ourselves in the societal mirrors — the posture and attitude of the spirit that, in my opinion, produces a wonder which is joyous.

For joy is the synthesis of the very young child's capacity to live socially — to perform in history — and the adult's capacity for self-awareness that little children have not yet acquired. Joy is rooted in an appreciation of the marvelous human paradox that is the relationship between social indeterminacy (the freedom to create ourselves anew, continuously) and societal self-identity (the certainty of knowing who we are); it is a spiritual experience located not necessarily in some other-worldly Heaven but in the human-produced sphere where history and society flow (not always very smoothly and never predictably) together.

Getting pleasure and giving joy

Pleasure, in contrast to joy, is strictly societal. One way that the difference between joy and pleasure manifests itself is that joy is richer and lasts longer. But it's not just a quantitative thing. Hedonism — the pleasure principle of principles that dominates our culture — has to do with getting as much as possible from life. Which is fine, in my view, if and when you can do it without hurting yourself or other people in the process.

However, the role determined, means-to-an-end, un-thinking behavior of trying to get something for yourself by coercing other people in subtle and not-so-subtle ways to give it to you — behavior which most of us have been taught is what we must do to have anything — often makes the pleasure principle difficult to live by in a culture such as ours, whose other dominating principle (of pre-capitalist origins) is Judeo-Christian religious morality. Being our brother's keeper, doing unto others as we would have them do unto us, finding it more blessed to give than to receive...these are extremely difficult to reconcile with the acquisitional, greed-driven hedonism that's urged on us every time we turn on the television set or open a magazine.

While joy, in my view, lies in savoring the paradox of social indeterminacy/self-identity, the irreconcilable contradiction between religiosity and hedonism that is a defining characteristic of Western culture is tremendously painful; indeed, it can be spiritually deadening. Many people in our culture don't even try to reconcile the contradiction; they simply dedicate themselves to being the best getters they can possibly be, telling themselves and anyone else who wants to know that at least they're not hypocrites. Perhaps that's true. Then there are those people, considerably fewer in number, who decide not to have anything in their lives rather than to live at the expense of other human beings; they settle for deprivation in the belief that the negation of getting is at least morally superior to selfishness. Perhaps it is, in a world where those are the only choices.

In my view, however, giving — more than getting — creates other possibilities; it opens the door to development, as well as to joy.

In *Let's Develop!* I tried to show what it is to be giving, emotionally, in a culture of getting. What I mean by such giving is the active sharing with other people of all our emotional "possessions" — including, in the appropriate environments, our pathology, our pain and our humiliation. The point is not that getting is bad. It's simply that as the highly rule governed, culturally prescribed behavior associated with societal roles and institutions, getting sometimes gets in the way of development.

The reinitiation of development

Just as the development of very young children is initiated through performance — imitating who they aren't — performance is how development can be reinitiated at any point in life.

Contrary to what traditional Psychology has to say on the subject, lifelong, unlimited development is not only possible but natural and healthful. When people stop developing, it's not because they've reached their limits but because they're no longer engaged in the kind of performatory life activities that allow them to go beyond themselves; they stop being in (building) environments where they're being supported to do what they don't know how to do, so all they can do is what they already know — acting out the same societal roles, over and over again. Viewed this way, Psychology is not so much a science as a self-fulfilling prophecy.

I wrote *Let's Develop!* as a workbook, with exercises at the end of each chapter that are designed to help people step out of those roles by performing as who they're not — and in doing so to live their lives as an ongoing exercise in development.

In our culture of getting, the societal rules and roles require that we invest most of our emotional and spiritual energy in trying to get as much as we can; men are supposed to give as little as possible, while women are taught to give only in order to get. (Although the roles of men and women have undoubtedly changed over the last 25 years, I believe the evidence is overwhelming that, in the words of an old song, "As time goes by...It's still the same old story..." for the vast majority of people in our culture.)

A life that's lived in accordance with the pleasure-getting principle is so rule governed and role determined that there's little room in it for development. When you make giving the organizing principle of your life, however, you're self-consciously choosing how and who you are — which is why the more giving you are, the more developmental your life is likely to be.

In the absence of development, joy is unlikely to come into the picture; when people are overly bound by societal rules, when they're boxed into societal roles, they have no sense that they're choosing how they live for the simple reason that they're not. They're trapped in their lives without necessarily even being aware that they are. They don't know that there's an alternative; they go through life thinking that this is just "how it is" — a singularly joyless experience.

On the other hand, development doesn't guarantee joy. Then what's the point of development? There isn't one, in the sense that development isn't a means to an end. It doesn't get you anywhere. It isn't *for* anything in particular — a better love life, children who do their homework, a cure for cancer. A developmental life opens up possibilities — it gives you more choices, in big matters and small ones — but asking the development question doesn't automatically produce the "right" answer; it doesn't define what you do (or how you do it). It still leaves open the question of what choices you make (which may be more or less life-enhancing), as well as the question of what attitude you bring to the activity of making them.

This is how it's possible for people to be developing and still not be living joyfully. Development may be a necessary condition for living, in this sense, but it's usually not sufficient. It's not just that there's "more to life" than development, quantitatively speaking. I'm talking here about the quality of life; what *kind* of life are you creating/performing? For just as a highly skilled artist can nevertheless make uninteresting choices of what to paint, it's also possible to make life choices as if you're fulfilling a duty, or because it's the "psychologically correct" way to live. Or you can allow yourself to be exhilarated by the activity of choosing, to experience the freedom that comes with living your life developmentally.

This is what it is to relish the unique human paradox of being located in the unity that is history and society; you can relate to life as an adventure, a play that you're creating as you live it. Or not.

Critics and fans: Two sides of the same societal assumption

Alan and Lee, both high school teachers in their early forties, have been in therapy with me for several years. Alan is married and has two teenage children; Lee is divorced. The two of them are good friends — it was Alan who suggested that Lee come into social therapy when his marriage was ending. Both are intelligent, kind, outgoing men who are successful in their careers and have people in their lives they care deeply about and who care deeply about them — me being one of those people. Yet neither Alan nor Lee is living very joyfully.

Alan, who wanted to be a teacher all his life, says he can't even imagine himself doing any other kind of work. He has a strong sense of what the totality of his life — his historical performance — is about. Yet he's often unhappy with the look of his day to day life; he's like those movie critics who obsessively and compulsively find fault with everything, from the casting to the dialogue to the scenery.

Lee used to be an executive in the insurance industry; he made a lot of money, lived life in the fast lane, and was completely miserable. He says teaching "saved" him, and he's highly appreciative of what his life looks like now. But he has very little sense of life as a whole — he's hardly aware that there is such a thing as history, still less of his connection to it. Lee tends to be indifferent to what's happening beyond what he can see in the societal mirrors; he's like a moviegoer who's so involved in the action on the screen that he's oblivious to where he is, how he got there, the people sitting near him, and what he'll do when the credits come on.

Of course many people go to the movies like Alan does, or Lee. Think of your friends the obsessive critics, who love to point out all the things that the movie you just saw together did wrong from the vantage point of "reality." Think of your other friends, the fanatic fans, who have crushes on the actors and seem to believe that what they see on the screen *is* "reality."

Critics and fans alike are caught up in the myth that in order to enjoy a movie — indeed, to have any artistic experience at all — it's necessary to be "carried away" by it, to be persuaded by the "make-believe." Some professional thinkers about the theatre have even made up a rule on the subject; they say that people who watch a play have to engage in a "willing suspension of disbelief" — that is, members of the audience have to agree to act as if it's possible for someone to age 40 years in two hours, or for a battle to take place on a "battlefield" the size of a large living room, or for lovers to carry on a "secret" affair despite the presence of hundreds of people who see them make love night after night.

But art, like everything else in life, is only what it is: a painting or a tap dance, a drum solo or a piece of sculpture, a poem or a symphony. It may be absolutely wonderful, or quite mediocre, but why should we need to "believe in" art to appreciate it any more than we need to "believe in" a sweater to feel its warmth? It's simply one of the many, many things that we human beings create, neither more nor less real than anything else. Nor, for that matter, is it more or less illusory.

The critics, who have little appreciation for society, and the fans, who lack a sense of history, both fail to experience (give themselves to) the dynamic *relationship* between social-historical species life and the individual self; historical performance and societal appearance; indeterminacy and identity; activity and behavior; being and illusion.

Rather than behave in the societally prescribed role of the critic or the fan, you can watch a movie as who you are: delighting in the illusions that flash before you on the screen, fully aware that you're in a theatre in a neighborhood on a street — in the world, along with every other human being who ever was or will be.

To be without a sense of history, as Lee is — to know yourself only as you appear in the societal mirrors, to take that illusion as something other than an illusion, to let the illusion be all that you can or want to see — is an expression of *narcissism*, Narcissus being the name of that very handsome young man of ancient Greek myth who fell hopelessly in love with his own reflection. It is a lonely and terribly undernourished way to live. On the other hand, to have *only* a sense of history and no appreciation for day to day, moment to moment societal life, like Alan, is to be "out of it" in every way, and often in a great deal of pain — as those modern mythological creatures called "Revolutionaries" so often are.

While both Alan and Lee have chosen how they want to live, they aren't fully savoring the choices they've made. They may be living their lives developmentally, but there's not much joy for either of them in doing so. In his own way, each tends to see the cup of life as half empty rather than half full.

Alan, in fact, seems to be waiting for something dreadful to happen: illness, failure, loss and, inevitably, death. He watches himself getting older and sees only what he's losing (his hair, his 20-20 vision, his energy) rather than what *is* there. Does "the worst" — which people like Alan are always expecting — ever happen? All the time. But no one ever cheats death, tragedy, aging, or even ordinary mistakes by being preoccupied with the possibility that they might occur (or "knowing" that they will). Ironically, people like Alan — who often pride themselves on being "realistic" — actually can't see what they're doing very clearly through the dark lenses of their pessimism and their cynicism. They rarely experience the joy that comes from continuously choosing to do what they do.

Judgmentalism versus joyousness

Many people have judgments about joy. There are those who just don't believe in it; for religious or moral reasons they may feel that joy is a kind of emotional extravagance that's an expression of self-indulgence, or worse. Others have simply never thought of joy as something to want; they have a passive attitude toward life which often gets expressed as relief that nothing terrible has happened. In other words, some people think that joy is "beneath" them, while others feel that it's more than they have a right to expect.

Sometimes children are taught to make such judgments by an authority figure in their lives, who in turn got his or her ideas from an even higher authority — perhaps Dr. Freud, Dr. Spock, or the Bible. When such children grow up, they cling to "their" judgments without even being aware that they have them, or where the judgments came from. This is how it is that so many people live their lives deprivationally, even miserably, assuming without necessarily saying in so many words that this is the right way to live or the only way to live.

You may know people who seem to have everything going for them and yet don't get much out of what they have. And you may know others who don't have that much, materially or otherwise, but they're living joyously nevertheless. They use what they do have to enhance their lives…something that many people have never learned how to do, or perhaps don't believe in doing. You see this very clearly when two people are in similar, even identical, circumstances — a husband and a wife, neighbors, co-workers — and one of them is passionately involved in the choreographing of his or her life, while the other is going through the motions, more or less politely but with one eye always on the checkbook or the clock, and wondering: "How much is this costing me?" "When will this be over?" and "What's the point?"

Yes, human beings can eat just to keep ourselves alive, without bothering about the taste, texture, look or smell of the food we consume. And we can also survive on an emotional diet that's designed not for joy but simply to keep us going. The trouble is that when you're eating simply for survival, or having sex just because you or someone else has "gotta" have it, you tend to do those things almost without noticing that you're doing them, still less how; you don't give much thought, or anything else, to those activities. Which turns out to be rather joyless for you and the people you're doing them with.

Unlike pleasure, which is all about getting, joy is all about giving. It's a positive attitude that you bring to life: being glad that you've chosen to do what you're doing with your life as a whole, whatever that may be — bringing up children, doing work that you care about, devoting yourself to a good cause — and at the same time allowing yourself to be constantly touched, intrigued, challenged, inspired, and surprised by how that choice is manifested and expressed in the hurly-burly and the humdrum of everyday life.

I don't believe that there is such a thing as "the right way," or "the only way," to live. However, I do think there's a whole lot more to give to life than simply trying to get through it. Just as we may breathe, eat, walk, sleep, do sex, watch a movie, go to work and clean the house joylessly, we can learn to do all of those things in ways that enhance and enrich life. Why bother? Because of all the things it's possible to do with life — besides getting through it, you can also explain it, search for the "meaning" of it, avoid it or spend it dreading the moment when it will be over — what makes the most sense to me is to live it, as joyously as you can. Which means giving your all to it, whatever you have, all of the time.

What's the idea?

As human beings we do not merely live. For at least the last 2,500 years, we've been reflecting on our life process as we engage in it; that is, human beings produce ideas out of our material existence — our life activity. It's unlikely that we would have been doing so from the moment human life began, about a million years ago, since our species not only evolves but (unlike any other) develops. Over the millennia, however, what it is to be human has come to be inseparable from our extraordinary gift — which no other species appears (of course, from *our* point of view) to possess — for self-consciousness and the creation of ideas.

The ideas that we derive from life take many, many different forms: representations, theories, judgments, interpretations, analyses, dreams, categories, models, values. Art, science, religion, philosophy, myth, and law are a few of the names we give to the various kinds of ideas people invent. No society regards every kind of idea as being equivalent in worth to every other; for about the last 300 years in Western culture, ideas that attain the status of "science" are placed higher in the hierarchy of ideas than those labeled "art," or "religion." Moreover, ideas — like other human inventions — have histories; some which started out as "scientific theories" were later reduced to the level of "superstition" or "prejudice," while others that first appeared as "science fiction" (an art form) eventually became "scientific facts."

Humanity's most splendid achievements — everything from the sculpture of Benin, the poetry of Tu Fu and Mozart's sonatas to the printing press, antibiotics, the fuel-driven engine and the legal presumption of innocence — are the results, in part, of our capacity to produce ideas. At the same time the manipulation of that unique human capacity has resulted in some very terrible products — genocide, slavery, war, racism, sexism, exploitation, and oppression among them. No other species can claim to have created anything remotely comparable to the music of Charlie Parker or Ludwig van Beethoven, and no other species need acknowledge enormities such as the burning of "witches" at the stake. Neither the grandeur nor the baseness is more, or less, human than the other; we are capable of, and responsible for, both.

It is our remarkable capacity to create ideas which gives rise to idealism. I am not using the word *idealism,* as it is frequently used, to mean the "naivete" typically associated with people who are called "do-gooders" and "dreamers" (to distinguish them from those who are said to be "cynics"). Nor am I referring simply to the philosophical perspective known as

"Idealism." Rather, I am speaking of idealism as a normal habit of day to day life in our society. Itself an extremely powerful idea in Western culture, reaching into the most remote corners of human experience, idealism is the attitude that attributes to ideas a privileged status; the everyday idealist regards ideas not as human inventions produced from the raw material of the life process, but as Things that are independent of, prior to, and more fundamental (more real, more important, more valuable) — in a word, *larger* — than life.

In other words, idealism is a way of being in the world which mistakenly takes the illusion that appears in the societal mirrors to be all that there is; idealism "forgets" the activity — the performance on the stage of history — that ideas merely reflect in a particular light. In contemporary culture this substitution of the image for the imagining, which is part of the historical practice of life, has come to dominate how we are and how we see ourselves as well as everything else.

> *The school psychologist tells Mr. and Mrs. D. that their seven-year-old son is hyperactive, suffers from low self-esteem and attention deficit disorder, and has a borderline IQ.*
>
> *Eric feels humiliated when his wife receives a promotion that comes with a higher salary than he earns.*
>
> *Margaret wishes she could find a bathing suit that will conceal her fat thighs.*
>
> *Mrs. F. disapproves of the fact that her son and daughter-in-law take separate vacations.*
>
> *Jack is disappointed because the woman he hopes to marry doesn't want to have children.*
>
> *Sharon believes that if her former fiance had really loved her he wouldn't have had an affair with another woman.*

Pauline says that at 70 she is too old to travel.

Ron knows that the reason he hits his children when he's had too much to drink is that his father was an alcoholic who was often abusive to his family.

Larraine, Ron's wife, understands that she tolerates his behavior because she has a dependency problem of her own.

These are among the myriad commonplace forms that idealism takes. In such situations and countless others, most of us allow ourselves to be ruled by culturally/historically produced but now disembodied ideas: labels; judgments about what is right, beautiful, good, normal, and true; assumptions; explanations; knowledge. It is not merely that we believe, devoutly and as a matter of course, in this or that idea. Idealizing — labeling, judging, assuming, explaining, knowing — becomes how we organize our relationship to life; we distance ourselves from the process, the creative activity, of performing in history, devoting our energy instead to having ideas (judgments, assumptions, knowledge) about it; we forget where these ideas come from. This systematic misuse of our marvelous capacity for self-consciousness is the source of much emotional pain in our culture.

It's as if a great artist were to abandon the love of his life because he has become infatuated with the beautiful portrait he himself painted of her. A tragedy? An absurdity? An act of madness? Yes, all of those…and yet not altogether uncommon, incomprehensible, or even surprising. For our gift of self-consciousness — the human capacity to create ideas from life and in doing so to go "beyond" ourselves — carries with it the potential for deadly and deadening idealism.

As very young children, human beings learn all kinds of things. In doing so we learn, also, that we are learners and that we are learning. And we learn that there are things to be learned. In learning our ABC's, for example, we also learn that we are learning the letters of the alphabet and that there is such a thing as the alphabet to be learned.

That we come to perceive the processes we're involved in is, I believe, what makes human speech possible. Remember the very young child, just learning to speak, making noises to which older children and adults respond? The baby babbles, other people talk back to and with the little one — and in this social activity, this *relational* form of life, a moment arrives when it dawns on the child that he or she is making noises, something which turns out to be...speaking! That is, the child's noises emerge into speech simultaneously with the emergence of self-consciousness, through the process of participating with other human beings in the social activity that is speaking.

In this environment, as very young children we discover ourselves in the moment that we see ourselves to be doing a quite wonderful thing; we learn, "in retrospect," that we've been asking for a cookie, saying bye-bye, announcing that it's time to go to the potty, telling other people who we are and where we live and that we're sorry.

What we "naturally" infer, in our essentially dualistic culture, is that if we learned something then there must be (or must have been) something that we learned — that is, some *thing* "out there" to which the piece of learning corresponds. And, "naturally," we conclude from this that language must be about something, must refer to something, must denote something. This is no mere philosophical blunder; it's not surprising that we should allow meaning — the significance we give to the ideas constructed from our experience of speaking — to overtake and ultimately obliterate language-making and meaning-making as *activity*. Yet while the inclination to do so is completely understandable and appears to be perfectly natural, it's also entirely mistaken. Moreover, the mistake of idealism is very, very costly.

Our capacity to create ideas from our experience — our ability to go beyond ourselves — makes not only the acquisition of language but all other development possible. Yet our tendency to substitute the ideas thus generated for life activity itself prevents us from having new kinds of experiences by overdetermining and constraining our ongoing involvement in life processes. If we define subsequent experiences in terms of the categories, assumptions, judgments, and understandings that we already possess in the form of ideas derived from what has gone before, then we're doomed to discover only instantiations of what we already know. What irony! The same gift of self-consciousness that has so enhanced human life impoverishes and diminishes us when it is used, as it frequently is in our culture, to stifle our continued development.

"High" tragedy, "low" comedy...it's simply life

Some years ago, the 13-year-old son of my next-door neighbors was killed in a car accident. On the evening of the day that Timmy was buried I sat with Tim, his father, in their living room. Friends and relatives had brought over food, and after a while Tim began eating a sandwich. In a low, shamed voice he murmured to me: "You know, Fred, people are nothing but animals. If anyone had ever told me that something like this could happen to one of my kids and I would still be hungry, I wouldn't have believed it. But look at me — my son is dead and I'm sitting here eating."

Tim was disgusted with himself for having the ordinary urge to eat that evening, believing that such a tragic moment ought to have driven out every need, every desire, while grief took over his body and his soul. Many people, like Tim, are governed by the idea that Tragedy (like Art, or Sex) is debased when everyday life is allowed to touch it; they assume that in order to experience grief, to appreciate beauty, to feel passion, in ways that are appropriate to these "higher" emotions they must have them in a pure form, on another plane, out of this world. Yet it seems to me that it is their allegiance to idealism which, ironically, prevents them from giving full expression to their emotionality. My friend Tim allowed the idea of Tragedy to impose upon and substitute itself for the tragic experience of Timmy's death; the father's grief was distorted by his shame at not grieving in the right way — as the idea of Tragedy dictates that we do it.

Certainly there are distinctions between things: subtle, barely perceptible differences of nuance as well as differences of considerable magnitude. Yes, there is tragedy. There is art. There is sex. But it isn't necessary to enter an exalted state of being, a higher plane, to "have" them. They are moments not truly separated (nor separable) from the most prosaic and utterly mundane moments with which, intertwined, they make up the rich totality of life. Notwithstanding the ideas we have about life, in life itself the ordinary and the extra-ordinary, the ridiculous and the sublime, the most banal and the most profound, are continuously at play with one another; they are like the colors on an artist's palette which have run together so that it is impossible to say precisely where that shade of blue-green, or that brownish-red, begins and ends.

To force the various moments of life apart, as idealism does in glorifying the categorizing, labeling, and judging of them — regardless of whether it's done in the name of Science, Ideology, Religion, Therapy, or any other ideal authority — is profoundly non-developmental and unjoyous.

It is a denial and a violation of the human spirit to divide ourselves from ourselves, as if we were no different from objects made up of parts that can be detached from the whole. For it is the irreducible paradox of human life, it seems to me, that our humanity lies precisely in our capacity to be profoundly self-conscious of our utter banality.

Interestingly, the individuated self — among the most powerful ideas ever generated by Western culture, one which is associated with some very valuable contributions to human development as well as with very terrible atrocities — is not required for self-consciousness. Quite the contrary: transfixed by the illusory image (the idea) of the self in the societal mirrors, we absent ourselves — our social selves — from the stage of history where life is performed. Rather than living history in the recognition that it will, perhaps, judge us, we attribute to ourselves the right to pass judgment on it (just as certain religious authorities presume to know what God "thinks" and "wants").

Indeed, it is in our capacity for *self-consciousness* that I believe human spirituality resides — and not in the ultimately *self-serving* promotion of idealizations such as the self that, however fascinating, beautiful, and moving they may be, are after all merely (albeit magnificently) the products of our own creativity, our own imagination, our own invention.

It's what you do that counts

The trouble with idealism — or perhaps more accurately, if less idiomatically, idea-ism — in everyday life is that it gets in the way of living joyously. It is a cultural cancer afflicting virtually everyone. Lost in their ideas and judgments about life — the illusory images which appear in the societal mirrors — practicing idealists rarely find themselves in that joyful place where society and history come, at times very abruptly and conflictedly, together.

When Elaine looks at her 70-year-old mother, for example, all she sees is a self-centered, selfish woman who can never be forgiven for failing to live up to the idea Elaine once had of her. "To me she was the nicest, prettiest, best mother in the world," Elaine recalled one evening in therapy. "I used to walk around thinking how lucky I was to be her little girl."

Elaine remembers Betty, then in her twenties, as an adoring Mommy who was lavish with hugs and kisses, smiles, and surprises; a Mommy who never came back from a shopping trip downtown without bringing a present for her "sweetheart," took Elaine and her cousins to the movies most Saturday afternoons, was always ready to play a game or tell a story, and — having taught Elaine to read before she was four — delighted in showing off her bright, adorable child to visiting relatives.

But by the time Elaine was 14 or 15 years old and three younger children had come along, that Mommy had disappeared; in her place Elaine recalls a moody, aloof, inexplicably angry Mother who often ridiculed and sometimes beat her oldest daughter for being "lazy," "dirty," and "spoiled rotten."

To this day, Elaine still relates to Betty as if they were both characters in a fairy tale with an unhappy ending. The story that a highly imaginative, rather lonely child made up about her life has become the grown-up Elaine's memory (which is neither "true" nor "false," but an idealized recollection) of their life together. For memories — no less than photographs, dreams, novels, operas, and animated cartoons — are only impressions taken from life; they may be more or less creative, more or less interesting, but they aren't identical with the historical performance of life itself.

Elaine's insistence on identifying Betty, and herself, with the idealized characters (and corresponding judgments) in the story of her childhood makes it very difficult for them to create something new together as the actual (historical) human beings that they now are. As flat, two-dimensional, ahistorical characters, they're unable to give one another very much; they exchange the tokens of familial affection and politeness which have societal value and significance — holiday visits, birthday presents, phone calls at regular intervals — but there's little intimacy, still less joy, in their relationship.

Elaine is like someone who goes to a dance only to spend all her time in the ladies' room seated in front of the mirror, criticizing the reflections of herself and anyone else who comes in, then going home without even having heard the music. Perhaps she gets some satisfaction from thinking that at least she knows who had the nicest dress, the weirdest hairdo, the most expensive perfume, the worst figure. But joy only comes from getting your body — with all of its limitations, and however awkward or tired or stiff you may feel — out there onto the dance floor with everyone else while the band's playing and the crowd's swaying: trying out the latest steps, doing what you do with flair, gettin' down, swinging your partner or dancing cheek to cheek — and catching a historical glimpse of yourself going beyond yourself in the mirrors on the wall as you dance by.

Don't I know you?

Refusing to be with Betty in history, Elaine encounters her mother only as the illusion which appears in the societal mirror that is The Family: Elaine is the Hurt, Resentful Daughter; Betty the Hurt, Guilty Mother. Constrained by those societally determined roles, they're finished products who by

definition can only do what they already know how to do —
over and over again.

As a consequence, Elaine assumes she knows "everything
there is to know" about her mother. But that can only be if
what Elaine means by "knowing" is possessing idealized information about the societally overdetermined particulars of
Betty's life.

Certainly, it's possible for one person to use such information about someone else to manipulate and exercise control
over him or her. You may even be able to predict what another
person will do on the basis of having these "facts of life" in
your possession. But in my opinion, the only things worth
knowing about another human being are what you learn in the
activity of building something together, whatever that may be:
a car, a conversation, a business, a relationship, a life.

For what we create is an extension — a continuation, a
completion — of ourselves. Whatever you and I produce
together is neither completely you (yours) nor completely me
(mine); it's us (ours). In producing it we're engaged in the
ongoing relational activity of producing/learning who we are.
What I mean by knowing is not a passive state of mind that corresponds to something which we assume must exist "out there"
if it is "here in our heads" (as the traditional picture of knowing
suggests), but a creative, collective, ongoing, active, and constantly emergent *process*. When people make something with
each other, they thereby have a many-textured connection to it
that includes comprehending what they've made and the other
human beings with whom they've made it and who, by virtue of
doing so, are part of it. In the absence of building something
with people, you miss the uniquely human dimension of them
as producers. You may see them as they appear societally, but
you can't be with them as who they are in history.

Like most other human beings, Betty is capable of all kinds of things: humor and bitterness, modesty and arrogance, generosity and selfishness, intelligence and stupidity, courage and cowardice — the whole gamut of human qualities and characteristics which find expression in complicated and ever-shifting ways that don't form any particular pattern at all. She's taken all that, along with the material and cultural and emotional circumstances in which she's found herself, and created her life with it — as all of us do; that's what it is to perform in history.

Betty's given some fine performances in her day; she's also fallen flat on her face. Most of the time, like the rest of us, she does what she can do with what she has available to her. Sometimes that works pretty well, and sometimes it doesn't. Unlike the creature of Elaine's childish imagination, Betty is neither the embodiment of the Good, nor of the Bad. She's simply — and complicatedly — an ordinary human being, much like everyone else, often surprising those who assume they know her best (including not only Elaine, but Betty herself).

One night not long ago Elaine talked in a social therapy group about having gone with Betty and Louis, Elaine's father, to the doctor's office to find out the results of some tests Louis had taken. The news was not good. Elaine's parents held hands as they listened to the doctor explain that the cancer was spreading and that Louis had, at best, another six months to live.

Elaine was full of reluctant admiration for how Betty handled this very difficult and painful moment. "My mother was like a different person," is how Elaine explained it to the group. "For once, she didn't try to grab all the attention. She didn't seem to be thinking of herself at all. She was everything

you'd want your best friend to be — straightforward, support-
ive, caring — completely there for my father, all the way."

Still, Elaine was critical of Betty. "Why does it take a life
and death situation for her to be that way? Why can't she ever
have an ordinary conversation with me, for instance, without
complaining or criticizing everyone and everything?"

Although I could understand what Elaine was saying, it
really doesn't make much sense. After all, hearing the doctor
say that the man you've been married to for more than 50 years
is going to die soon is very different from having an "ordinary"
conversation with your daughter. (For that matter, being the
carefree young mother of one precocious little girl is hardly the
same thing as being the going-on-40 mother of four.)

Why does Elaine expect Betty to conduct herself similarly
in such dissimilar situations, which actually have very little to
do with each other? Why does Elaine assume that because
Betty is "good" in one set of circumstances, she ought to be
"good" in the other — or even that she's trying to do the same
thing? After all, poets don't ordinarily balance their check-
books in verse. Nor are you likely to see a pastry chef baking
pies on the bus.

When I pointed this out, Elaine asked: "Are you saying
that dealing with a crisis is one of my mother's strengths?"

You could say that. But why does Elaine have to have a
name for what Betty, or anyone else, does? Why must it fall
into a category — in this case a "strength," the categorical
counterpart of "weakness" — that Elaine can admire or criti-
cize? Fortunately for everyone concerned, this very painful life
situation is the kind of thing Betty can handle. But as a human
being, a performer in history, she's not reducible to the labels
and categories that her oldest daughter uses to explain and
judge her.

Although Elaine does not formally practice any religion, she tends to view life in ahistorical, "eternal" terms: constantly comparing people with her ideas of right and wrong, categorizing them as good or bad, and rewarding or punishing them accordingly.

Did a "new" Betty suddenly come into being in the doctor's office that day, transformed by the impending death of her husband into still another overstated ideal — "everything you'd want your best friend to be"? I think it's more likely that in fact what changed was Elaine's *idea* of her mother (just as it was her idea of Betty that changed — the "fairy princess" becoming a "wicked witch" — when Elaine was 13 years old).

Many people in our culture share Elaine's tendency to confuse ideas with what they're about. This confusion is associated with the rarely questioned, idealistic assumption that everything has an explanation. We often invent ideas such as categories that are supposed to explain life, and then try to force life to fit inside them. When life activity asserts its emergent, unpredictable, indeterminate nature (as it is constantly doing), we're apt to insist that our ideas are "right" and life is "wrong" — overlooking the fact that the ideas are merely societal inventions formed from the raw material of life; life does not originate from them.

Elaine's committed to thinking that, *regardless of what Betty does*, she's "really" nothing other than Elaine's prefabricated idea of her: someone so preoccupied with herself that it takes a matter of life and death to jar her into ordinary decency.

Down with ideals!

I think that if Elaine is going to continue to grow, she has to confront her insistence on seeing her mother in terms of this fixed idea of Betty which Elaine's been carrying around all these years. Why is that a condition for growing (up) — not to mention living joyously? Because keeping Betty in *her* societally determined place/identity as a bad mother keeps Elaine in *her* societal place/identity as a helpless child who's only the passive object of Betty's love (or resentment). Elaine's idealism is stultifying to the development of both women; it's made both of them, mother and daughter, behave childishly, thereby robbing them of the possibility of living joyously (something only grownups can do).

Elaine told me that she thought I was right, "in theory." But she said it was hard for her to imagine that she could just stop making judgments when that's typically how she does thinking — not just about Betty, but about virtually everyone and everything else. I agreed.

It *is* unlikely that Elaine can just stop doing what she does, even if she's decided that she'd rather not do it. (That's rarely how it works, regardless of what it is that someone wants to stop.) I think Elaine needs to be engaged full-time in historical productive activity — building whatever she can build with other people. Does that mean Betty, also? It might, depending on whether the two of them choose to make something together.

That creative activity includes giving expression to the conflicted and often intense feelings that accompany such activity — feelings which are very different from the judgments that are produced by comparing life to the societally determined ideas we have about it. It isn't simply that the feelings are different in content from the judgments, although they are. Rather, "the expression of feelings" is a more giving activity which itself produces something new. The "having of idealized judgments" typically doesn't create anything; it's lifeless.

When I asked why she thought she needed ideals to live

by — why she couldn't simply live — Elaine, along with almost everyone else in the group, was shocked. "If you don't have ideals, you can't know whether you and other people are doing the right thing," she said. "I want to know if I'm a good person, and if the people around me are good."

But, even assuming it's possible, why does anyone need to know that? Why should we measure life against our ideas of Right and Wrong, Good and Bad (which are, after all, merely human-made societal constructs elevated to eternal Truths?) What about philosophizing, the creative, practical-critical activity of questioning such assumptions in the performance of our lives?

Making it

Neil and Natalie are longtime members of a couples therapy group. For the last 20 years they've been making things together — including their rather unusual marriage, their relationships with their two daughters, friendships that mean a great deal to each of them, and some very fine films about the impact of war on the lives of ordinary people.

They come to therapy not because they have problems they're trying to solve, but because they like "working out" in the philosophical environment of the social therapy group. Which isn't to say that Neil and Natalie are the perfect couple, or that their marriage was made in Heaven. They're ordinary people who simply work extra-ordinarily hard to make whatever they make. And they're quite happy to have a little help from their friends.

When Neil and Natalie met, she was already known for her remarkable book of photographs of Vietnam; he was an entertainment lawyer working — less than happily — for a major Hollywood studio. To Neil, Natalie's work was not simply wonderful but important. He saw immediately that her pictures enabled her to speak on behalf of people who could not speak for themselves, which had always been Natalie's dream; this became Neil's dream as well. It was Neil's idea that Natalie should make films, because she could reach a larger audience that way. He became her business manager and eventually her partner; they married some years later.

Neil says he understood from the beginning that if he and Natalie were going to make a life together, he had to let her go — meaning that she had to be free to pursue her dream, wherever it took her. Neil's never backed down from that commitment; he wants passionately for Natalie's work to be seen. And he's willing to give her everything he has to make that possible.

Natalie spends much of her time working, even when she's not on the road. At home, she's often in the studio that they had built next door to their house so she could have the space to work undisturbed. Neil spends a lot of his time with their daughters. He and the girls, who are 14 and 17, often invite friends over to eat dinner and watch a movie with them; they're all avid sports fans who never miss an opportunity to watch their teams play in person.

Natalie's included in what they're doing whether she's physically present or not. The idea of a Wife and Mother may require that she be with them, but Neil and the girls don't need her to be; they want Natalie as who she is. Nor does Natalie feel the need to be the only person in their lives who can "really" be giving to them. Natalie wants Neil and their daughters to have much more than that.

Is Natalie ever afraid that Neil might someday want to be with someone else? She says she doesn't worry about it; over the years there have always been other people Neil's preferred

to be with at particular moments and for particular reasons —
colleagues, friends, their daughters — and she's never felt
deprived by it so the idea of it doesn't disturb her. Moreover,
to go around dreading the possibility that Neil might fall in
love with another woman — perhaps someone who would be
more like a "real" wife to him, someone younger, prettier, less
independent — would be to deny what she and Neil are actually doing together.

Looked at in a certain societal way, Neil may appear to be just
a fool (or an opportunist) who's living in the shadow (or the
reflected glory) of a brilliant woman. And Natalie may seem to
be merely a nut (or a charlatan) who believes (or says she
believes) that she can singlehandedly right the world's wrongs
with her camera. And perhaps their relationship, viewed in the
light of societal judgments and expectations, looks like a '60s-
style "open" marriage in which the "liberated" partners are
"doing their own thing" according to the principle of "live and
let live."

Certainly there's not much resemblance between the life
Neil and Natalie have made and the idea of a Good Marriage
which most of us — including the two of them — have been
taught to believe in. Deciding to live together as they do, without relying on such ideas and assumptions to overdetermine
their life, was a big decision. They both take it seriously; a lot
of intense work goes into the day to day production of a life
that's something other than a reproduction of societal ideals.
It's an exhilarating, creative, strenuous activity, which is not at
all easy for either of them.

But it's how they've chosen to live. And when they look in
the societal mirrors, they like what they see reflected there: a
happily married couple with children they love deeply, living a

materially comfortable life; a prize-winning artist and a talented businessman whose partnership has succeeded in doing some good in the world; an outgoing, caring man and a deeply intelligent woman who are part of a circle of close friends.

Neil is Natalie's closest friend, and she is his. But they don't do what they do with each other because they're Best Friends; their friendship is a product of the life activity in which they both participate. Intensely engaged in the activity of living their lives, they have a strong sense of themselves and one another as builders. Who these two people are to each other is what they're doing: building a life together, which includes the work that Natalie does to make the world more decent and humane, and bringing up their two daughters to contribute to such a world. Together they are living their dream — performing the imperfect, improvisational play that is their lives, and joyously savoring every scene of that sublimely human comedy.

Living your dream

In our culture, where idealism is the dominant mode of belief, many people tend to assume that joy is contingent on the possession of ideals — persons or things or experiences that conform to the culturally received ideas of what they should be. But since these perfect and permanent objects are also, by definition, unattainable, we're taught to "outgrow" the desire to live joyously. (This is what's typically meant by being "realistic.") Instead, we're encouraged to acquire as much as we can get…even if it isn't very fulfilling or meaningful. (This is what's usually identified as being "materialistic.")

In fact, neither realism nor materialism is opposed to idealism; realism is an attitude toward life that recognizes ideals as belonging to another realm or plane of being and "reality" as the world of the here and now in which we're more or less forced to exist; materialism is the attempt to bridge the gap between the ideal and the real through the accumulation of less-than-perfect and temporary objects.

Materialists and idealists, longing for unattainable ideals, rarely live their dreams. Occasionally, what they settle for is wonderful: kindness, peace, comfort. Certainly, kindness and peace are precious, rare; their value, in my view, is often not appreciated enough. And surely every human being has the right to a comfortable life. If that's "all" people have, they're tremendously fortunate. The question is whether the *condition* for having them is agreeing to give up the pursuit of your dream — perhaps without even being aware of what the dream is. For it often turns out that in giving up the possibility of living your dream, you compromise the very way of life that you got in exchange for it. Kindness can come to seem intrusive. Peace may eventually resemble mere politeness. Comfort sometimes becomes stultifying. You could decide, having given up your dream, not to give anything else. And then life is joyless indeed.

But how do you know where the pursuit of your dream may lead — especially if you don't know what it is? the realist may demand. That's like asking what a play is about, or where it takes place, or whether it has a happy ending, before it's been created; no one can say. Is that a problem? I don't think so. On the contrary, that's the joy of it!

I happen not to believe in an other-worldly dimension where ideals reside. In my view, it's the historical activity (what Wittgenstein called "forms of life") that we create with one another which is what there is. And joy, it seems to me, is to be found in the ongoing performance of that activity on the historical stage as we simultaneously, self-consciously, view ourselves performing in the societal mirrors; it's seeing ourselves living our dreams, whatever they turn out to be.

Give up my ideals! you may be thinking. *Is that necessary to live a joyous life?*

Yes! In my opinion, it is.

Living my dream! you may be wondering. *That sounds wonderful, but isn't it also scary?*

Yes! In my experience, it's wonderfully terrifying and terrifyingly wonderful.

Learn to philosophize! you may be worrying. *Are you saying that anybody can?*

Yes! It's not a matter of knowing how, but performing as who you aren't.

Perform! you may be grimacing. *Even if I've got two left feet, a tin ear, no talent?*

Yes! It's what you have to give to the *Performance of a Lifetime*.

Okay...but hamburgers in history! you may want to say to me. *Isn't that a little far out, Fred?*

Yes! And, like joy, it's also very near at hand.

II

THE UNITY OF LEARNING, DEVELOPING, PHILOSOPHIZING, PERFORMING, AND JOY: A COMPLETION

L *earn, develop, philosophize, perform...joy?* Many people might find it hard to put these words into the same sentence without also including phrases such as "never could," "too late now," "not for me," "highfalutin' hogwash" and "chocolate in all its forms." It's even harder for many people to imagine that the uniquely human activities of learning, developing, philosophizing, performing, and experiencing joy could possibly be related in any way. Yet learning, developing, philosophizing, and performing comprise a unity of activity that I believe is necessary for living joyously.

The fact that learning, developing, philosophizing and performing aren't supposed to have anything at all to do with joyousness is, in my view, not simply unfortunate; rather, I think this is among the many tragedies of our contemporary culture. For in the absence of learning developmentally and performing philosophizing, it seems to me most unlikely that we can ever experience joy. And few people know how to philosophize or how to perform — or, for that matter, how to do *the kind of learning that produces development.*

TWO KINDS OF LEARNING

To notice that neither philosophizing nor performing are national pastimes is likely to strike most people as an unremarkable observation. Now that I've called your attention to this fact of societal life, you may be thinking: *Yes, and so what?*

After all, as I pointed out in Section I, in our culture philosophizing is largely identified with that obscure, not very popular, dead or near-dead academic subject called Philosophy. Abstract, irrelevant and useless, Philosophy is generally regarded as the exclusive possession of professional philosophers, not an ordinary life activity. Not surprisingly, given what Philosophy is, few people are able — or inclined — to philosophize. The same is true of performing; although considerably more popular, it too is carried out in our culture mostly by professionals — in this case, professional actors.

But to say that *learning* is similarly unpopular and exclusive may seem to be, on the face of it, absurd. Aren't we living in the Age of Information? Doesn't the Information Superhighway originate here? Hasn't the American Dream been transformed from "a chicken in every pot" to "a computer in every classroom"? Isn't everything that's ever been written now available on CD-ROM? Aren't we all on our way to an E-mail address? Perhaps.

But the acquisition of information and the complex skills required to manipulate it successfully — which is, if not *the* national pastime, at least one of those sports which is very big business in America — is not at all the same as genuine (that is, developmental) learning. Indeed, in contemporary society the activity of learning has been systematically overtaken and replaced by the behavior of accumulating and manipulating information — so much so that we have come to think that knowing (having) things, and the skill of using what we already know to generate more and more things, are the whole point, and proof, of learning.

That is, learning is largely defined in terms of knowing — the means-to-an-end accumulation of quantifiable information and skills that can easily be tested, measured, and exchanged for something of societal value: a grade, a high school diploma or a college degree, a professional certification, a driver's license. Lev Vygotsky contrasted this societal tool-*for*-result, instrumentalist behavior of acquiring information and skills with what he called "the only learning worthy of the name": learning that leads development, a tool-*and*-result historical creative activity which only human beings do.

The point is not that the acquisition of information, and the skills to manipulate it, are "bad." Like the societal behavior that results in having money, with which it is closely connected, having such knowledge and know-how can be quite useful. As you go about your daily life, it's convenient to have acquired all sorts of information (hot water comes from the left-hand tap; an eight-ounce glass won't hold a pint of orange juice; when the big hand is on the 3 and the little hand is on the 8, it's time to leave for work; how much change you need for the bus; what the symbols "Third Avenue" on a street sign signify) and skills (ironing a silk shirt; programming the VCR; balancing your checkbook; reading a newspaper to find out how your team is doing in the playoffs or how the stock market is behaving)...and that's even before you arrive at your job, where you need to have a million other facts as well as skills at your command. So yes — having information and skills, like having money, makes good societal sense.

What *is* problematic, in my opinion, is not the acquisition of information and skills, but identifying that tool-for-result, necessary societal behavior with the equally necessary tool-and-result historical performatory activity of learning that leads development. For acquiring information and skills, while it contributes to the stability and continuity of everyday life, is by virtue of that very fact both limited and limiting; it has little to do with development. As we acquire more information and skills, we don't thereby become someone new; we simply assimilate these new possessions into the societal categories and structures of knowing that are already there. In doing so we may enhance ourselves in our societal location, but not in our historical one. The acquisition of information and skills doesn't necessarily lead to qualitative transformation, or growth. It is an alternative to, not a substitute for, learning that leads development.

Todd and his wife Barbara, for example, both in their early thirties, are very accomplished "knowers." A specialist in international business law, Todd works in the overseas investment department of a major bank; Barbara is the vice president of an executive search firm. They're so good at (overidentified with) knowing that they have no idea how to learn developmentally, which requires doing what you don't know how to do.

Picture this scene. Todd and Barbara, who've been married for less than a year, are in bed together. In the last several months they've had sexual intercourse once or twice; most times Todd has been unable to have an erection. Tonight is another one of those nights.

The evening started out alright: Barbara picked Todd up after work, they got something to eat and then went to a movie they'd both been wanting to see. But Todd couldn't help worrying about what would happen later — now it *is* happening, again. *Impotent!* The word flashes through his mind, over and over, like a blinking neon sign. Barbara tries to arouse him, but after a while Todd tells her to stop. "It's not happening," he says apologetically. "I think I'm just wiped." He kisses her on the forehead and turns away. "How about going to sleep?" The last thing he wants to do is to talk about "the problem" with her.

But Barbara wants to talk. She's sure there must be some explanation — and a solution. The other night she had asked him if he was seeing someone else. No! Todd had told her angrily. Was he having second thoughts about the marriage? No! he'd said again, hoping she'd leave him alone. Tonight she's urging him to see a doctor, someone who specializes in "these things." Todd tells her she's being ridiculous — he just had a complete physical exam. Still, he wonders if maybe there might be something wrong with him physically. What else could it be? The truth is that Todd doesn't know what's going on, or why.

Nor does he know what Barbara means when she says that they could have sex "another way," but he hasn't told her that he doesn't know and has no intention of doing so. He *can't* ask her. He can't ask anyone. Besides, what is there to know? He's a grown man, he's had other relationships. Of course he knows! As Todd sees it, there *is* no "other way." There's what you do beforehand ("foreplay" in his high school health and hygiene textbook; the kids called it "fooling around"). But that's not the same thing as sex...

Meanwhile, Barbara has begun to talk about Todd's mother, who killed herself when Todd was six years old. Barbara's analysis: Todd is taking out his anger at his mother on her. Todd interrupts her. "It's three in the morning. I'm sorry you're disappointed. We can talk about it another time if you want to. But I've got to get some sleep now."

Hurt and resentful, Barbara gets out of bed and storms into the living room, where Todd can hear her crying. He's disgusted with himself, furious with Barbara, and unbearably lonely. Like many people in our culture who feel compelled to play "the knowing game" in their bedrooms, Todd sees himself as a loser.

Since information/skill-getting is a matter of adding more of the same to what we already have, and since knowing often brings with it substantial societal rewards, you might expect that it would be easy to do. Not at all. For in the almost complete absence of developmental learning, many people in our culture find acquiring new information and skills a terribly painful experience; tedious, coercive, and humiliating. Moreover, it's often unsuccessful. Remember what it was like to "learn" geometry in school? French? History?

The awful mix of boredom and anxiety which so many people associate with school (and with after-school lessons that were no less agonizing for being "extracurricular") is characteristic of tool-for-result learning, even for adults who have made a self-conscious decision to acquire certain societally valued information and skills. Whether you're a first-year law student at a prestigious university, a woman whose husband is teaching you to drive, an accountant studying to become certified, or a father-to-be enrolled in a natural childbirth course, you are likely to experience some form of the emotional dis-ease which often accompanies learning that is overdetermined by the dominant acquisitional learning model.

This is the model that prevails in our public schools, largely defining what learning is in our culture. Some children manage to acquire the information and skills they're required to know (at least for long enough to pass a test) but many, many never do.

Picture this scene. Eight-year-old Keith, a third grader, is listening to his teacher as she reviews what the class is supposed to know about multiplication. She has explained it all before, but Keith still doesn't quite know what the multiplication table is (although he is aware that he is supposed to know). Obediently, he writes his name on the test paper and looks at the first problem: *Six children are coming to Gloria's birthday party. If each child gets three brownies, how many should Gloria's grandpa bake?* Keith thinks: "Okay. That makes seven kids. Seven times one is seven, seven times two is 14, seven times three is..." Now what? He can't remember what Mrs. Davis told him yesterday. He has no idea how to go about this thing. Nor, for that matter (and not surprisingly), does he have much interest in doing so. He's about to glance over at Petey's desk for a clue, but Mrs. Davis is looking his way; the last thing he needs is for her to accuse him of cheating. Keith feels stupid, frustrated, ashamed, and angry. Wishing he could somehow disappear, he imagines himself playing basketball with his 14-year-old cousin Tony. For a moment, Keith is pleasurably caught up in remembering what Tony, an up-and-coming forward on his junior high school team, said last

Saturday afternoon when he taught Keith how to dribble the ball: "Hey, Mr. K! You're catching up to me!" Suddenly, Mrs. Davis is scolding Keith for daydreaming again; no doubt a conference with his parents is on the agenda.

The adults in his life are convinced there's something wrong with Keith. The teacher and the school psychologist use terms like "attention-deficit hyperactivity disorder" and "learning disabled" to explain what the problem is. Keith's parents are disturbed by the suggestion that he be put on medication, but they don't know what else to do. Keith isn't a "bad" child. His I.Q. tests show he's "normal." So why won't he *learn*? How will he get through school? How will he get into college? And without a college degree, what kind of future can he hope to have?

That Keith is merely an inexperienced mathematician (in the way that very young children are inexperienced speakers) who is quite capable of developing as a mathematician (in the way that young children develop as speakers) has simply never occurred to anyone. The prevailing information/skill-based approach to teaching children requires that they be related to almost exclusively as having a relatively fixed identity (a child is either a good knower or a bad knower), so there's little room in it for relating to them as who they can become. And that's true regardless of *what* label is applied to them, whether it's "gifted," "developmentally delayed," "learning disabled," or anything else. So school, ironically, is not a place where children are likely to develop as learners. (It's a good thing children don't learn to speak in school, some people have said — otherwise they might never learn how!)

Some of us come out of school knowing more, some less. The best knowers, those who have acquired the most information and who can show what they know to the teacher on a test or in a report, earn the top grades. Eventually, they will get into the most prestigious colleges, from which they will some-day graduate to the highest-paying jobs. Few people in our culture, whether they've been identified as good or bad at knowing, know how to do learning that leads development — the learning that very young children do long before they ever get to school and even before they have any idea that there are such things as learning and knowing.

The dominant model of learning, which valorizes know-ing/showing that you have information and skills at the expense of learning that leads development, doesn't only dominate officially designated educational settings. At the office or the cocktail party, in the bedroom or the bowling alley, the prizes also go to those who have — or appear to have — all the answers; asking for help is out of the question. Sadly, the anxiety and humiliation that Keith experiences in the classroom do not get left behind there; for many adults, like Todd and Barbara, the emotional pain produced by having to know (and knowing to have) is woven into the fabric of every-day life.

Baby talk

The acquisition of information and skills is supposed to go on inside the head of the individual knower. This is what makes "cheating" reprehensible in traditional educational settings. This is how it is that once children begin to internalize the dominant model (it happens quite early), they become pas-sionately concerned to do things by themselves and for them-selves — which in our culture is valued very highly indeed.

This is why so many adults are exceedingly reluctant to ask other people for help in circumstances when doing it on their own — whether the "it" is choosing a new suit, dealing with a migraine headache, giving a dinner party, looking for a job, or starting a love affair — is precisely what intensifies the difficulty, pain, anxiety, or anguish they experience. People who conduct their lives in this way may "live and learn" in the sense that they have more information or skills than they did before, but the process through which they come to know what they know is non-developmental — to a large extent by virtue of being so thoroughly individuated.

By contrast, learning that leads development is profoundly social. It takes place in what Vygotsky called a *zone of proximal development* ("zpd" for short). Although it may sound like a place (an end zone, a tropical zone, a no-parking zone), the zpd is actually a particular kind of complex social activity that human beings (and, so far as we know, only human beings) do/create together: building the zpd. They do this not as a means to an end, which is how we do all sorts of other things — putting up a tent at a campsite, going to work, getting a haircut, bringing the cat to the vet, reading the instructions that came with the new vacuum cleaner, making reservations at a restaurant, studying a driver's manual, following a recipe, taking vitamins. Unlike such tool-for-result societal behavior, the historical activity of building the zpd is a tool *and* a result; the doing of it is both the condition for and the purpose of continuing to do it. In other words, what matters in the zpd is the process of production itself rather than what might or might not be produced by it (a conversation, an orgasm, laughter, a trophy, a paycheck, or anything else).

Another characteristic feature of the zpd is that the people who participate in building it are at various levels of development, ability, or experience. To use Vygotskian language, the zpd is a joint activity in which people who are more experienced support those who are less experienced to do what they don't know how to do. In the zpd, where learning is social, "cheating" — or, more accurately, "completing" — is what it's all about.

The classic example of such a joint activity is the zpd of early childhood in which babies learn to speak by participating with more experienced speakers in an "ensemble performance" of speaking.

Meet Jennie, who at the age of 10 months hasn't been around very long and is therefore inexperienced in speaking — as she is in just about everything else. Right now she's sitting in her high chair with nothing on the tray in front of her but some crumbs from the cookie she's just eaten. "Ku...Ku," says Jennie. She does so (as far as anyone can tell) not knowing precisely what she means by it, that she means anything at all by it, or even what meaning means. Jennie doesn't know much at all. She's simply making noises, like the grownups do. (The grownups, of course, see themselves as doing something quite different from simply making noises.)

Mommy, a more experienced speaker (just as Keith's cousin Tony is a more experienced basketball player) plays a "language game" with her: "Cookie? You want another cookie, Jen?"

Together, these two human beings — one a speaker with 27 years of experience, the other brand new to the world — are engaged in the joint activity of speaking. Jennie is performing speaking by imitating Mommy, thereby "going beyond" what she could possibly do "on her own." And Mommy, as Vygotsky put it, is relating to Jennie as being "a head taller than she is" by having a conversation with her child before Jennie is capable of saying something like: "I want another cookie. Please stop washing those dishes for just a minute and give me one — and if it's not too much trouble, could you make it chocolate chip this time?" That is, the experienced speaker is *completing* ("cheating") for the inexperienced speaker by accepting whatever Jennie does and taking it further. It is by participating in this social process with Mommy and others that Jennie is learning, *in advance of her development*, to speak. If she were only allowed to do what she already knows how to do, if Mommy and other people refused to talk to her until she got it right, it is unlikely that Jennie would ever learn to speak at all.

Now meet Justin, two years old. At a family gathering, Justin's Daddy asks the little boy to say his ABC's for everyone. Justin responds with a rousing rendition of the alphabet song, starting off with a thumping "A, B, C…" He stops for a moment, unsure of what to do next. "D, E…," Daddy sings in a soft voice. Justin joins him, finishing in a triumphant burst of "YXWZ!" Grandparents, aunts, uncles, and cousins all laugh and clap appreciatively.

And here's three-year-old Bobby, running into the living room to show his big sister his latest work of art — a sheet of paper covered with orange, green and purple scribbles. When Bobby tells her that it's a picture of her, 11-year-old Lauren is delighted. "Thank you!" she exclaims, giving the little artist a hug. "It's beautiful! And you even gave me a hat to match my roller blades, didn't you? I'm going to hang this up on my wall right now!"

What matters in each of these scenes is the *activity* — speaking, saying the alphabet, drawing — and not whether Jennie, Justin and Bobby are doing it the right way. They aren't corrected, criticized or punished when they get something "wrong" — Mommy doesn't tell Jennie she left out a verb when she asked for a cookie; Daddy doesn't insist that Justin recite the alphabet five times because he forgot what comes after "c" and jumbled the last few letters; Lauren doesn't take away Bobby's crayons because the picture he drew doesn't look like it's supposed to. Jennie, Justin and Bobby aren't required to know the rules of grammar or perspective before they're allowed to speak or draw. No...Mommy, Daddy and Lauren are doing what adults and older children often do with very young children — supporting them to do what they don't know how to do, and building on (completing) whatever they do. This is the remarkable social environment/activity in which human beings learn to talk, to walk, to dress, and to do all sorts of other things that make it possible for us to participate competently and knowledgeably in societal life. In other words, non-adaptive historical performatory activity — doing things that we don't know how to do, things that we couldn't possibly know how to do — is, ironically, what we have to do (in the first place) in order to become adapted to society.

The greater irony, the tragic irony, is that once the societally necessary task of adaptation is accomplished, the developmental process tends to get more and more closed down. That is, the historical performatory activity of learning leading development which makes societal adaptation possible is abandoned, making further growth impossible; the family, the school, and the other institutions "freeze" us in our societal places — our new-found identities — so that we're unable to move or to change in ways that are coherent with how the world is changing.

Identity (as in "fixed identity") is especially problematic at the present moment, when the world is changing with such extreme rapidity. Identity — the adaptation to how things are right now — becomes a form of maladaptation when it is divorced from development, given the abruptness with which things are constantly becoming very different from how they were five years ago, last year, yesterday. This is how it happens that these days, children in our culture very often know more about our world than grownups do — which can be a source of tremendous conflict between children and their parents and teachers, grownups whose identity is often centered on the societal illusion that they are the ones who know best.

One of the things that children know which grownups don't — or don't want to acknowledge — is that much of the information and many of the skills which their parents and teachers have acquired are outmoded or irrelevant. (Think of all the things you were required to know when you were a youngster, such as the "facts" of world geography and "good penmanship," which have gone the way of the dodo bird.) So children, not surprisingly, are less than eager to have them. Consequently, it's very difficult for these grownups who are overdetermined by the role of knower and the rules of knowing to teach children what they know that *is* of value. And it's virtually impossible for such grownups to learn from children; their identity as knowers doesn't allow them to do so.

Grownups (and older children) can learn as babies do

Todd came into social therapy with me soon after Barbara left him. In the first session we did together, he told me that he didn't "believe in" therapy. He was there, he said, because a friend whose opinion he respected had urged him to come and — since he knew he was "in pretty bad shape" — he had decided to see if I had any answers for him. "I feel like a jerk a million times over," he told me. "I couldn't get it up and I didn't know what to do about it. Then my wife left me…I can't seem to handle that, either."

A few months ago Todd joined a social therapy group. He

finds himself in a zone of proximal emotional development where he is supported to go beyond himself: a man virtually imprisoned in his identity as a Man Who Knows What He's Doing. In the social therapy group, Todd participates with other people in a creative activity to which knowing is irrelevant. Not having to know, he is free to imitate the members of the group who are emotionally more experienced and skilled than he is and to be completed by them. He isn't required to know how to do what they are all doing together before he can participate. And neither he nor anyone else is supposed to come up with an explanation or an analysis of what his "problem" is if he doesn't do it the right way. Like the other members of the group, he simply does what he can do and the group (including Todd) makes something with whatever that is.

In the bedroom, an almost exclusively societal zone where the preservation of identity/dignity/secrets requires people to behave according to the rules and roles that they came in with, Todd is compelled to do only what he already knows how to do: to cover up his humiliation and his pain with anger. Here in the historical "zped" Todd can perform as who he isn't; in doing so he is learning to be giving. (Todd recently suggested to Barbara that she come into social therapy — "no strings attached." She told him that she wasn't interested; she already knows, she said, what there is to know about being giving.)

Now watch Keith and his friends on the basketball court, where they are participating in a zpd that includes Keith's cousin Tony. Keith and the younger boys study every move that Tony makes; they notice how he stands, where his arms are when he dribbles the ball, the placement of each finger. They imitate him as closely as they can. At eight, most of them are considerably less mature than 14-year-old Tony is; their hands are smaller than his; they don't have the same muscular strength or eye-hand coordination. And they're all a lot less experienced at playing basketball. But Tony relates to them as basketball players, which is what makes it possible for them to learn in advance of their development.

Keith *wants* to be as good as Tony. He practices for hours, days, months on end; he rarely feels discouraged; he takes everything that Tony tells him about his game with utmost seriousness. "Attention-deficit hyperactivity disorder?" On the basketball court, Keith is capable of intense concentration for extended periods of time. "Learning disabled?" Here in the "zpbd" ("b" is for basketball), where learning leads development, Keith is a very good learner indeed.

In school, where learning is overidentified with and overdetermined by the acquisition of information and skills, Keith (like millions of other youngsters) just doesn't get it. The school environment becomes increasingly coercive — kids are bribed, bullied, threatened, and intimidated into acquiring information and skills — but they don't learn how to learn; they don't learn developmentally.

It's in this context of institutionalized failure and coercion that computers have come to be viewed as a solution to the crisis in public education. The neo-Vygotskian psychologist Michael Cole and his colleagues at the Laboratory for Comparative Human Cognition at the University of California in San Diego, for example, are in the forefront of a movement among progressive educators to place computers in public school classrooms throughout the country; they argue that computers can help children — especially those labeled "learning disabled" — to realize their potential to learn.

The implication, of course, is that computers are better at doing this than teachers are. Tragically, that's probably true. There could be no more telling critique, in my view, of the anti-developmental, and consequently anti-human and inhumane, environment which prevails in all too many of our schools than the fact that *in such an environment* machines are indeed superior to human beings at helping kids to acquire information and skills; machines, for example, typically do not blame, coerce, ridicule, or punish.

I greatly appreciate the computer because this extraordinary human invention is so useful for the information/skill-getting enterprise. It's not simply that computers give us access to much more information, much more quickly, than most of us are capable of getting on our own without them. Of much greater significance, in my opinion, is the fact that computers are highly effective as instructors in the dominant societal paradigm, or model, of information/skill acquisition. Children taught by computers, for example, don't merely acquire information; they internalize the method of means-to-an-end, tool-for-result learning required to be a good knower. In fact, I think there is strong evidence to support the argument made by a growing number of educators during the last 25 years that children — particularly the ever-growing numbers of them who fail to learn from teachers in traditional classroom settings — are best taught this sort of learning by computers.

Unlike those people who would like to rid the world of these marvelous machines because they disapprove of how they are sometimes used, I believe very strongly that everyone should have equal access to computer technology. In my view, there's no more reason to throw out computers on the grounds that they can be misused than there is to stop giving people antibiotics because we believe that the institution of Medicine is organized in such a way so that drugs are sometimes misused.

Wonderful as computers are, however, they can *only*

enhance our ability to acquire information and skills; they don't enable us to do the kind of learning that leads development. Which is not to say that, after all, there really is something wrong with computers. These machines simply are what they are; they're neither more (better) nor less (worse) than that.

The stopping of development: An unnatural disaster

It's at about the time they enter school that most people in our culture stop being supported to do what they don't know how to do. The zpd of early childhood, the historical "theatre" where human beings perform as who we aren't and in doing so continuously create ourselves, is dismantled. It is replaced by that set of societal mirrors I talked about earlier, in which we can only see who we already are: "difficult," "bright," "shy," "stubborn," "slow," "cooperative." According to the accepted wisdom, this array of cognitive and personality characteristics — our developed "identity" — supposedly stays with us all of our lives and largely determines what we're able to learn, know, and do.

There are all sorts of pseudo-scientific explanations for the fact that in our culture many, perhaps most, children stop developing soon after they enter school. Indeed, in my opinion what it *means* to grow up in our society is to stop developing. The playfulness and risk-taking — the babbling and bumbling — of creative imitation that characterize the very young child's performance in the zpd are considered inappropriate in older children and adolescents; when adults engage in such unknowing activities, it is frequently taken as a sign of immaturity, emotional illness, or mental retardation.

According to traditional Psychology, that human development should grind to a halt is "normal." I call it a disaster. It is not, in my opinion, a natural disaster, but a human-made one which is terribly damaging to all of us as individuals, as Americans, and as members of the human species.

At home as well as in school, the learning that leads development characteristic of the zpd is all too soon shunted aside in favor of the individuated, behavioristic model of acquiring (and displaying) information and skills called "knowing." By the time Jennie is five, Mommy will tell her to stop being "silly" when the little girl playfully makes up her own words for things. In the first grade, Justin will be reprimanded for copying a word from another child's spelling test. At seven, Bobby will be expected to draw "real" pictures. In a variety of situations, parents and teachers will say to them: "You know better." "Act your age." "You're not a baby any more." "That's only for big boys." "No, you're not old enough." "Don't touch that…you don't know how to use it."

Despite the fact that as very little children they learned all kinds of things by performing what they didn't know how to do, they will soon discover that now what matters most is knowing, and showing that they know, how to do things the right way. In school they will be tested regularly to see whether they know what children of their age ought to know — that is, whether they are at their grade level, above or below it — and they will be diagnosed and treated accordingly.

Throughout their school years, Jennie, Justin and Bobby will be expected to acquire more and more information and skills. But none of what they will get to know is supposed to lead to any qualitative transformation of who they are; indeed, such acquisitional societal learning behavior is completely divorced from the historical activity of development.

Which is why being in school is, for many, many children, such an ungratifying, uninteresting, even excruciating experience. Can the difference between how Keith is on the basketball court and how he is in the classroom be explained by saying that basketball is inherently fascinating and fun while multiplication is inherently dull and difficult? I don't think so. (Indeed, when basketball is taught in school or at summer camp by means of traditional school methods, it is often as difficult and painful for children to learn as math.) In the classroom, a purely societal environment where he's required to acquire information because it is "good" for him, it's no wonder that Keith's attention wanders! If there's a "disorder" here, in my opinion, it's in the coercive, inhumane societal institution of the school — not in the human being who's being coerced and dehumanized by it.

By contrast, the environment in which Keith is learning to play basketball is a bona fide zpd. On the court, Keith experiences the joy which is to be found at the juncture where history and society meet. Performing, he's in the same (historical) league as Magic Johnson, Larry Bird, Air Jordan, and his other heroes; he's also old enough to be able to watch himself performing: an eight-year-old boy who, while far less experienced and skilled than they are, is nevertheless playing the same game that these great athletes play.

Todd has that experience of joyousness in the social therapy group. Performing, he's creating (culture) in history along with every human being who's ever lived or will live; at the same time, he's able to appreciate the remarkable fact of his performance: an ordinary man who is helping to build an extraordinary environment in which people, including himself, can give expression to their fears, their pain, and their passion.

For adults only

The very youngest children aren't yet capable of experiencing joy, nor do they "need" to; they perform in history without reflecting on the fact that they are doing so, the "meaning" of their performance, or anything else. They simply haven't been in society long enough to be able to perceive themselves performing. That is, they *can't* be self-conscious because they haven't had time to acquire that quintessential societal possession: a full-blown self. In this existential situation of self-lessness from which we all start out, we do not require a resolution of the contradiction between the two central facts of post-early childhood human life: the historical fact of our freedom to create everything there is, including our nature, and the societal fact that we are determined by what we create.

At the beginning, unencumbered by the oppressive self-identity that the various societal institutions will soon impose on them, very young children are free to go beyond themselves continuously. From moment to moment, day after day, month after month, they babble, tumble, topple and bumble their way into societal life. How do they sound? How do they look? How do they smell? How are they doing? They don't (can't) know, or care! This marvelous freedom to play without rules is something that children exercise without being aware that they are doing so. For they have no "depth," no notion of who they are; the youngest children perform unself-consciously because there is as yet no self, no image, to be conscious of. The absence of self-consciousness which characterizes early childhood is a precondition for doing the learning that leads development.

What I mean by performing, as very young children do it, is what Vygotsky called *playing*. The games that they play, unlike the games played by older children and adults, aren't governed by rules that the child knows beforehand; rather, the rules emerge (if they emerge at all) in the activity of playing the game. The most important of these games are like the "language games" that Wittgenstein created to show the historical dimension of language as a relational activity that human beings do together. In the language games of early childhood, what matters most is not the content of what is being spoken (what the words already mean or represent) but the social activity of speaking itself — a "form of life."

As the weeks and months and years go by, Jennie will become a better and better player of language games (as well as all kinds of other societal games) even as she is becoming conscious of herself as such. Gradually, the loosely rule governed meanings of language (its societal uses) will come to take precedence over language as relational activity, so much so that Jennie — like everyone else in our culture — will become more or less oblivious to the historical performatory dimension of language acquisition. In fact, it's highly unlikely that she — any more than most other people — will ever come to be philosophically aware of herself as someone who not only uses the prefabricated meanings that we all receive as part of the process through which we are adapted to the societal *institution* of Language, but who once participated with other human beings in making meaning as part of the social/historical *activity* that language originally is.

To have an adult awareness of ourselves as being simultaneously historical makers and societal users of meaning (culture) requires that we be able to philosophize. Yet the societal institutions — including Language itself — are adamantly opposed to our doing so. Like every other societal institution, Language disguises its origins in historical, performatory, relational activity; it presents itself to us instead as a pre-existing, natural phenomenon. It's not a conspiracy — just how things are. As very young children we're unable to perceive the actual developmental process through which we learn language; later on, as adults, we're typically compelled by the societal institutions to forget it. Most of us become increasingly sophisticated users of language while remaining utterly unsophisticated about the fact that what we are doing is engaging in the activity of language — in a form of life.

It is one of the many ironies of human life that the lack of self-consciousness in young children — an absence which makes it not only impossible but unnecessary for them to appreciate themselves as performers — is the very thing that holds adults back from performing. For as we become sufficiently adapted to be able to see ourselves in the societal mirrors, we simultaneously get caught up in the illusory image of ourselves — the self-identity — that appears in them.

That is, the self which is produced in the historical performatory process through which we become adapted to society comes to stand in the way of performance later on. For while there is no self for the very young child to see, adults find it exceedingly difficult to see anything other than themselves. It is the stultifying self-consciousness (the ego-centrism) of adulthood which keeps us from performing in the way that the youngest children do — not because they choose, or desire, to perform; it's simply what they do, given that they're little children.

That very young children have no selves of which to be conscious ("to speak of") is the precondition for their participation in the various zpd's of early childhood (such as language acquisition), where learning leads development. However, adults in our culture are very definitely "self-possessed."

But being self-conscious doesn't mean that adults can't engage in learning that leads development. We aren't babies, but we can imitate what very young children do *as who we are* (self-conscious adults) just as they imitate us as who *they* are (unself-conscious little children). Philosophizing — a language game for adults — is what allows us to perform as children do, given that we aren't children. We're not children, but we can be child-like.

Learning how to philosophize requires that we perform — the *performance of philosophizing* that's like 10-month-old Jennie's performance of speaking and two-year-old Justin's performance of saying the alphabet and three-year-old Bobby's performance of drawing. We're child-like when we're performing. We're child-like when we're philosophizing. We're most child-like when we're performing philosophizing: asking big questions about little things, something that we don't know how to do — or why.

The point here is not that philosophizing is a good thing in and of itself. It's simply that since we, as adults, confront an existential crisis as a consequence of our self-consciousness, it's a good thing that we're able to philosophize — which is the only way I know out of that crisis into history. It is our capacity to philosophize which allows us to comprehend ourselves historically, and thereby to discover the joyousness at the juncture of history and society. Joy (like despair), in my opinion, is something which only adult human beings, who are simultaneously the producers and the product of our collective life, *can* experience. We create/discover it by engaging in the learning-leading-development activity of performing philosophizing.

"Philosophize? I don't know how!" protests the self-conscious adult, unwilling to appear stupid. "Perform? I have no talent!" objects the self-conscious adult, reluctant to look foolish. "Imitate? Go beyond myself? Be who I'm not? That's phony!" frowns the self-conscious adult, clinging to the societal illusion of identity.

But if we're going to philosophize, we'll *have* to do what we don't know how to do. And yes, that's what performance is

— being who we aren't, going beyond ourselves, imitating. Is that phony? Not unless you insist on believing that the images which appear in the societal mirrors are the "real" (and only "real") you.

Such performances are profoundly social; they take place in "theatres" (in this case, zones of proximal philosophical development) — environments that people build together where they are supported to do what they don't know how to do (in this case, to philosophize). Perhaps you *will* look silly doing it, but...so what? You're only looking silly in the societal mirrors. There is no silliness — for we don't *appear* — in history; we're simply there.

PHILOSOPHICAL THERAPY

In social therapy groups, the task is to create a performatory philosophical environment where members of the group can self-consciously learn to play language games — in particular, language-of-emotions games.

"Language games," let me remind you, is what Wittgenstein called the philosophical exercises he invented to help clear away the "mental mist" surrounding the societal institution of Language (with a big "L"), so as to show that the speaking of language (with a small "l") is "a form of life." For Language, like every other institution, originates in the historical activity of human beings. It is only later on (in the life of our species *and* in the life of every individual) that it comes to be governed by societal rules, which overdetermine what it is. At first, however, there is no institution of Language; there is only the activity of language. Interestingly, both Wittgenstein and Vygotsky, in making this point, quote Goethe: *In the beginning was the deed.*

By analogy, our earliest human ancestors were in all likelihood eating before they imposed rules that in every culture overdetermines this life activity — just as in all cultures every individual, as a baby, eats long before knowing the right way to do it or even that there is such a thing as a "way" — right or wrong — to do it. Quite soon, however, the shared social experience of eating gives way to the rule governed institution of Eating. In becoming adapted to society, human beings acquire not only the behavior (such as using a knife and fork, the fingers of the right hand, or chopsticks) but the emotions (such as feeling disgust for whatever may be forbidden or unfamiliar) that give us our culturally drawn picture of what eating is; most of us find it exceedingly difficult to see or do eating otherwise.

And so it is with language. The distinguished contemporary psychologist John Shotter, following the Italian philosopher Vico (1668-1744), imagines that human beings may have discovered language during a collectively experienced thunderstorm or some other local earth-shattering event, to which they would have responded by making sounds and gestures as they ran away. Afterward, in retrospect, Shotter suggests, they might have come to associate the sounds with their shared social experience of danger; they learned that the sounds could be used to refer to, or mean, things (occurrences, objects, feelings). Eventually Language, with its institutionalized uses/meanings, was superimposed on the social activity of language (speaking) out of which it first emerged.

Similarly, very young children aren't seeking to convey meanings with the sounds that they utter. (Remember little Jennie, babbling away?) Rather, they are unself-consciously engaged in the joint activity of making meaning (playing non-rule governed language games) with other human beings. Later on they come to associate the sounds with that shared social experience, learning simultaneously that there is such a thing as meaning and that meanings have a use. In becoming adapted to the societal institution of Language, we lose sight of the meaning-making, poetic origins of language; as self-conscious adults most of us are far too constrained to perform language/make meaning/create poems.

That is, Language takes on a life of its own, becoming a thing-in-itself — a societal institution overidentified with the behavioristic *use* of meaning that's abstracted from the historical activity of *making meaning* which gave rise to it, so that what a word or phrase means is taken to be the same thing as how it is used. Such a picture of language as a system of exchangeable meanings (representations that stand for or are about the world in the way that currency represents the gold stored at Fort Knox) obscures the origins of language as activity, a relational form of life that human beings create together. When it comes to the language that we use to express emotions, for example, that picture of language overdetermines how we see and do our emotionality; it limits our capacity to develop emotionally.

Some scholars argue that Wittgenstein's purpose in creating language games was to show the identity of meaning and use. However, language does not originate in use but in the form of life that is the use-less, point-less, historical activity of meaning-making. While it may make societal sense to identify meaning with use, that identity only comes with the emergence of Language as a rule governed institution in which meanings are already fixed. Like making a poem (which is yet another form of life), the playing of language games doesn't simply affirm the societal nature of Language as use — it illustrates the historical nature of language as activity.

Language is fundamentally a complex form of life (or many forms of life). It doesn't come down from "on high" so that we can communicate; it emerges from the historical fact, the joint activity, of communication. This is what Wittgenstein's language games are designed to expose: the historical dimension of language that gets obscured by its societal uses/meanings. The language game strips away the metaphysics of Language — the institution's mystical, mythifying, ahistorical assumptions — to reveal its origins in the social interaction among actual human beings.

As a philosopher, Wittgenstein himself was engaged in a therapeutic enterprise. He wasn't trying to come up with general statements about the relationship between society and ideas (the sociology of knowledge), but to do clinical psychology with the professional philosophers whose "psychosis" stems from their "unnatural" attachment to Language. (It drives them to invent "essences," definitions, and other non-existent abstractions, and to spend their lives in tortured, futile pursuit of these figments of their own imagination.) In social therapy we play emotional-language games to cure ordinary people of their "neurosis," which stems from *their* "unnatural" attachment to Language. (Not being professional philosophers, their psychopathology is typically less severe.)

With the support of the social therapist, who is more experienced than they are in the activities of performing and philosophizing, people who are "in" social therapy engage in the ongoing process of creating a zone (a relationship) of proximal philosophical development where they can collectively question the myriad assumptions — in particular, assumptions about emotions — that overdetermine the ways in which they comprehend their feelings and conduct their lives. Some members of the group may have been doing this for years, while others are brand new to it. Together, they give an ensemble performance of philosophizing: the joint activity of deconstructing the societal constructions (scrutinizing the societal illusions) that limit how all of us are able to see, feel and be in the world.

Like all performatory historical activity (and unlike instrumentalist societal behavior), such philosophical questioning is not the means to an end; it is not a tool *for* a result, but a tool *and* a result. The joint activity of performing philosophy is how we create the non-instrumental environment in which the performance of philosophizing can go on — just as the joint activity of performing speaking is how human beings create the non-instrumental environment typical of early childhood, in which babies make meaning and thereby learn to speak. It is in this sense that the asking of philosophical questions — what we are doing, end-lessly, point-lessly, in social therapy — is not problem-solving, but the activity of creating culture.

That is, the social therapist is not a repository of philosophical, psychological, or any other kind of knowledge who possesses answers that members of the social therapy group are supposed to get. Nor is the social therapist, or anyone else, held up as a model — a person so "enlightened" or "advanced" as to be free of assumptions (something which may or may not be desirable but is certainly impossible). In social therapy we don't ask philosophical questions out of a desire to argue for argument's sake. We don't help people to "apply" the answers that the members of the group come up with (if they come up with any) to life. Social therapy is far more the making of a poem than the making of a point.

Aha! you may be saying to yourself. *Pointless activity! Just as I suspected! Then why bother asking philosophical questions at all?* That's a good philosophical question! After all, modern science, and the technology which grows out of it, have transformed the quality of life for billions of people by applying answers (solutions) to questions (problems). Societally speaking, it's perfectly reasonable tool-for-result behavior to ask questions from the vantage point of a consumer seeking to acquire a product (information). Consuming, however, has to do with using what's already there — not with creating something new. Consumption, after all, is not production; it isn't necessarily developmental.

What's critical for development (although not necessarily for Philosophy or Psychology) is *how* we go about seeking answers, rather than the what of the answers we come up with, if any. To scrutinize, actively and practically, our assumptions (that is, not just cognitively but emotionally, culturally and in every other way) — especially the ones that appear to go so deep they don't even look like assumptions at all — is very much a part of the developmental process.

For when we ask questions from the vantage point of not having to come up with answers — not simply questions to which no one (in the room, or in the world) yet knows the answers, but questions to which there may not be any answers to be known — we are engaged in a tool-and-result, creative, historical cultural activity. It is this performance of philosophizing which allows us to become reacquainted with the emergent (unpredictable, non-paradigmatic, unsystemized, unknown and perhaps unknowable) dimension of human life that distinguishes us from all other species.

In other words, questioning the unquestionable — a language game for grownups — is a reminder in practice of our historicalness; it diverts our gaze away from the societal mirrors and points in the direction of history. In asking philosophical questions, we see in a tool-and-result way that we *can* ask them; it jars us out of our usual way of seeing the world (including our assumptions about the world) as "just how things are" into the recognition that they can be *other* than how they are…if human beings choose to make them otherwise. The performance of philosophizing shows us that we're not simply the overdetermined products of our particular societal time and place, but also the collective producers of the totality of what produces us (including the societal assumptions of "time" and "place"). There is no point to this activity, no conclusion to be drawn; the social therapist is not seeking to replace "wrong" assumptions with "right" ones. Like the making of a poem, performing philosophizing/playing language games is a point-less, tool-and-result activity that frequently violates the rules of grammar, syntax, semantics and pragmatics, punctuation and usage, which govern normal discourse. In challenging those linguistic assumptions — in defining itself on its own terms, rather than relying on the external authority of the dictionary and usage to say what it means — the poem shows us that we are the historical makers as well as the societal users of meaning.

Similarly, the playing of emotional-language games challenges the assumption (what I have elsewhere called the myth of Psychology) that Emotions are gods, or even real — transcendant, ultimate Truths, first Causes, eternal and omnipotent states of mind. It thereby allows us, in a tool-and-result way, to see our emotionality (and our emotional discourse) as the human-made, relational, cultural artifacts that they are; that is, as forms of life.

It is this process, the self-conscious stepping away from societal safety and constraint for a moment into the boundless social-cultural spaces of history where there are no unchallenged assumptions (to hold on to or to hold us back), that opens up the possibility for adults to experience joyousness.

What is there to know?

One of the "deeper" and, in my opinion, more pernicious assumptions that's come to pervade Western culture over the last three centuries is that the universe, including everything in it, is knowable. This assumption is historically intertwined with the extraordinary accomplishments of modern science and technology, which themselves rest on two products of early Greek philosophy. One is the human being as observer/perceiver — a creature capable of viewing the world from a distance. (Descartes and the invention of telescopes and microscopes greatly enhanced this view and capacity.) The other, mathematics, the creation of which is traditionally attributed to Pythagoras, is a means of describing the rules (the laws of nature) that govern motion.

Closely related to the assumption that everything can be known is the assumption that the systematic acquisition of knowledge about the world is not only possible but necessary and desirable; such knowledge is the means, or instrument, by which human beings exercise control over nature. Accordingly, for the last 300 years or so (the modern era) the ultimate purpose of Science (the modernist deity) has been to know everything — that is, to come up with an answer for every what, where, when, how and why question that could possibly be asked.

According to a conception that emerged in Western Europe during the period known as the Enlightenment, "man" (all too often meaning the western/northern European man of property) possesses a natural, god-given ability to know and thereby control the world completely. As such he is made for this fully knowable world, and it is made for him. It was armed with this collective self-confidence — not to mention the deadliest weapons ever seen — that Western

European men took it upon themselves to conquer and colonize Asia, Africa and the Americas.

For hundreds of years, the assumptions which guided them have been critical in propelling forward the historically unprecedented accomplishments of Western science and technology. Everywhere in the world, human beings view the products of scientific achievement with respect, longing, and awe. Air conditioning, genetic engineering, space flight, microsurgery, fax machines, CD-ROM's — the control over and transformation of the natural universe made possible in part by the instrumentalist, cause-and-effect scientific paradigm have endowed the assumptions on which it is based with tremendous credibility and moral authority. This is so much the case that we no longer understand them as assumptions about the world but as how the world is. We're like those people who never take off their glasses; they forget that the glasses help them to see, but to see in a particular — a prescribed — way.

These days the Western scientific paradigm is the lens through which all of us look at the world, including ourselves. It too enables us to see in a particular way, and in doing so distorts and limits how we're able to see, to feel, to comprehend, and to live our lives. Why, for example, should we assume — as the scientific paradigm requires us to do — that it is always possible, necessary, or desirable to know the reasons, causes, or explanations for things? This is not to say that it is never possible or desirable to know why things happen as they do or how things are connected; if you drive a car, it's important to know how the steering wheel works and, perhaps, what its relationship is to the four wheels underneath. But what if the thing in question is a lover's infidelity? A child's fear of the dark? The desire to be alone? Can we know why? And even if it were possible, is it useful or desirable to know? I think it isn't, more often than not — considerably more often than the pseudo-science of Psychology would have us think.

Moreover, I believe that the unending pursuit of emotional explanations, causal connections, and reasons in the belief that such knowledge ultimately produces happiness — yet another form of the myth of (clinical) Psychology — is most likely to come to a spiritual dead end. Mired in societal assumptions, it cannot take us in the direction where, in my opinion, joy is to be found; it cannot take us into culture, the tangled juncture where history and society meet.

I am suggesting that we ask questions to which there aren't any answers. We can move along without knowing where we're going, without having a map, and create the route as we go — forward, if not toward a particular (pre-)destination. *How will we know when we get there?* you may be inclined to ask. Another interesting philosophical question. For if there is no "there," then there's no point to having knowledge/assumptions. *Is there an alternative to knowing?* Yes, historical activity: the self-conscious creation of culture.

From determinism to emergence

It's in the philosophical pause that's created when we stop to ask why, and how, we're doing what we're doing in the particular way we're doing it that we discover our historicalness — our uniquely human capacity to transform the very conditions, including our assumptions, which overdetermine who we are (our societal identity) and how we are (our societal behavior). This isn't to say that people necessarily act on that discovery; it simply creates the opportunity for them to do so by showing them that they can.

Imagine, for example, a world in which time didn't fly but

moved instead with excruciating slowness — a world where every moment seemed to go on forever. It's possible (or so it seems) in imagination, and perhaps in reality as well. Certainly it's highly unlikely that the beings who reside elsewhere in the universe, if there are any, would have days which lasted exactly 24 hours. Even if we were to be so biased as to translate everything into our own conceptions, we might at least imagine that their days go on for centuries (whatever *that* means).

Is such imagining completely frivolous? I don't think so. After all, this activity that we call life can be done (and conceived) in an infinite variety of ways. An interesting question, it seems to me, is why we choose to do it in the particular ways that we do. Why do we settle down, get diseases, look forward? Why do we fall in love, fear death, hate our enemies? Why do we feel depressed, humiliated, jealous, anxious? Why do we give names to things, talk about them, explain them? And why do we hold to the beliefs we have about ourselves that inform all of these activities and make sense of them?

To the extent that human life is viewed through the lens of determinism — the essentially scientific/religious conviction that it's possible to give a complete explanation or accounting for how we live our lives by invoking the presence of what is taken to be the ultimate causal factor (regardless of whether what's invoked is social class, fate, the gods, the genes, or anything else) — the question of why we hold to the assumptions that we do is less interesting and, perhaps, less relevant. From a deterministic point of view, the answer (the "be-cause") is already given in the laws of causation within a particular deterministic system. For the determinist, those assumptions are typically natural and ahistorical. That is, they are beyond the reach of human beings; our species' capacity to transform everything there is — our unique ability to create culture —

does not extend to these first causes. (If it did, then things wouldn't be determined.) However profoundly determinists of various persuasions may differ over what the fundamental laws of causation are, all determinists share the belief that the laws in which *they* believe are independent of human constructive activity.

A worldview according to which our lives are completely determined by *something* (whatever that may be) is therefore unlikely, ultimately, to have any room in it at all for human development, not to mention joy. Whether a man steals from his neighbor because their families are fated to be enemies, or because he belongs to a deviant subculture, or because he is evil, or because his father was a thief, makes no difference from the vantage point of development; overdetermined by one or another of such ultimate natural causes, he could not have done otherwise. Joyousness is similarly irrelevant to a deterministic worldview; if human beings are entirely determined to be only what we appear to be in society, then we cannot be or comprehend ourselves as the self-conscious historical creators of who we are. Such a deterministic worldview is antithetical to the radically developmental perspective that informs the social therapeutic approach, which is premised on the human capacity to create culture — to transform everything there is, including human nature itself.

The philosophical activity of challenging determinism is therefore critical, in the most practical sense, not only for development but for joy. It has everything to do with how we conduct our relationships with other people, how we work and play, how we go through our moments, hours and days, how we live our lives. That's why I think it's so important.

This is not to deny that causal factors — society, economics, culture, genetics — help to determine (with a small "d") who we are and how we live our lives. Obviously they do; we don't have wings, so we're unable to fly. It's simply that such factors aren't the whole story. What Determinism (with a big "D") leaves out is emergence, a crucial fact of human life which is anti-explanatory and non-causal; rather, it has to do with the unique evolution of something in a way that is not identical with, nor predictable from, nor reducible to, nor completely caused by, the factors that go into it.

The search for the missing causal link that will at long last explain us to ourselves in terms of the kind of laws that govern the movement of stars, the formation of mountains, and the reproduction of bacteria is a futile enterprise, in my opinion, in part because there is no evidence at all for the existence of such laws. Moreover, I believe it is fundamentally an anti-human enterprise (regardless of how the researchers may explain their motives to themselves and others). For to assume, as the pseudo-science of Psychology does, that its task is to discover the underlying logic, or pattern, which determines human life is to deny that we are not only societally determined but historically emergent — in other words, whatever patterns we discover are themselves the societal products of our unique freedom to determine how we live. I am not implying that what is typically meant by *reality* is "merely" a social construct, which would be like saying that the world is nothing but an ideal figment of our collective imagination. As a materialist, it's my opinion that the world is very much with us. What I am suggesting is that it's never "pure." For as the social constructionists argue, human beings are always and everywhere constantly giving form to it. Yes, the world is; it is what we collectively and continuously make of it.

To break with the centuries-old conception of an absolute determinism in favor of a point of view that includes all sorts of factors — one of them being emergence (which is in some ways the antithesis of determinism) — is to return, once again, to questions like: Why do we have the assumptions that we do? Where do our assumptions come from? Why do we cling to them as we do? How do they operate?

Asking such questions from an emergent point of view — that is, from the point of view that there aren't necessarily answers to them — is a different activity from the determinist's search for explanations. We ask them not simply to find out the origins of our assumptions. (Is it the Greeks? The Judeo-Christian religious tradition? The 19th century notion of progress? The mass media?) When we question our assumptions from an emergent point of view — when we ask why we conduct our lives as we do, even given the social-historical, material causes which prefigure them, and why our day to day life is as it is, and not otherwise — we are choosing not to capitulate to determinism but to challenge it...perhaps simply by ignoring it.

The assumption of dualism

Dualism, which is closely related in modernist thought to determinism, is a way of seeing (a picture of life) characterized by its insistence on the essential distinction between the observer and the thing observed. The dominant assumption in Western thought, dualism in its infinite manifestations (idealism being one of them) informs not only what we think about particular things but how we do thinking: Past and present. Night and day. Black and white. Cause and effect. Means and ends. Mind and matter. Spirit and flesh. Inner and outer. Thought and language. Form and content. The individual and society. The whole and its parts. Man and nature. Subjective and objective. Ideas and reality. You and I...

In Western culture we are taught to think it only natural to see the world in terms of these and other dualistic categories; most people find it exceedingly difficult to stand at any distance from the overarching dualistic framework, and thereby to view it as what it is: a human construct. Native speakers of English and the Western European languages tend to take it for granted that we use the dualistic terms we do because they have a particular kind of relationship with the dualistic reality we're describing: supposedly, such terms reflect or correspond to it.

"Reflection" and "correspondence," like "relationship" and "description," all belong to a family of terms which serve to bring back under the same conceptual roof (to re-connect) the seamless unity of life which dualism splits in two; in reconciling or mediating between the sides of the dichotomy, they serve to strengthen and perpetuate the assumption of dualism. (Academic exercises, such as the ever-present "compare" and "contrast," have a similar use.)

It's not simply that our vocabulary gives expression to a dualistically conceived universe; dualism is embedded in the very structure of our subject/predicate-based language, thereby overdetermining the form of our speaking as well as its content. According to grammatical convention, the necessary and sufficient condition for a declarative sentence — the "model" sentence in our language system — to be "complete" is that someone or something (a noun or a pronoun) acts, has acted, will act, may act (a verb form); the who/which is distinct and distinguishable from the doing. That is, the seamlessness of human life — the one-ness of historical activity — is excluded from our language not merely by verbal signs proclaiming "Stay Out!" but by the linguistic architecture itself, which has no room for life's unity.

Dualism pervades our moral and ethical discourse: our

religions, our courts, our psychology, our "common sense," all make judgments on the basis of "duals" such as good and evil, heaven and hell, sacred and profane, right and wrong, guilty and innocent, normal and abnormal. Dualism pervades our medical discourse: with the acquiescence of patients as well as doctors, diagnosis and treatment are carried out from inside the dualistic paradigm of sickness and health. Dualism pervades our cultural discourse: not only critics but the rest of us tacitly embrace the dualistic categories of life and art, fact and fiction, actors and audience, beautiful and ugly. So fundamental is the assumption of dualism that to question the categories which give expression to it seems almost bizarre. *Of course* there must be two (and only two) sides to every story; two (and only two) sexes; two (and only two) political parties.

The history of dualism

Difficult as it may be to imagine, dualism has not always been with us. Many of the pre-Socratic Greek philosophers — about 2,500 years ago they began asking big questions about little things and in doing so became the "founding fathers" of Western thought — were not dualists but monists. Pythagoras' semi-mystical theories of mathematics, for example, did not depend on observation, the seminal methodological conception which required the separation of the observer and the observed. Nor did the geometry of Euclid, who lived about a century after Socrates.

Interestingly, both Heraclitus and Parmenides, the pre-Socratic philosophers who have come down to us as the principal protagonists in the earliest known philosophical quarrel over which is fundamental, subjectivity or objectivity, change or permanence, nevertheless came to their different positions from a monistic perspective as well. Heraclitus argued that change is the essential characteristic of reality and that we know this because our experience of the world is constantly changing; it isn't possible, he pointed out, to step in the same river twice. But that experience is illusory, Parmenides replied. All we really have is permanence; the objective nature of the world is unchanging.

Over the next two centuries pre-Socratic philosophers of various persuasions conducted a series of such dialogues in which dualism did not enjoy a special status but was simply one point of view among others. It was the great achievement of Plato (speaking in Socrates' voice) to synthesize the opposing monistic views represented by Heraclitus and Parmenides into a dialectical dualistic system which (while not judging them equal) acknowledged the validity of both the "experience" of constant change and the "fact" of permanence, and showed how they were related. In a realm beyond the reach of ordinary human perception, said Plato, there exist unchanging, perfect, god-like Ideas of Truth, Beauty, Goodness and Justice, as well as lesser others. What seems to be reality — what we perceive, through our senses — are the transitory and flawed imitations of the Ideas, which are not knowable sensuously. However, the wisest of men (those who rise above the common attachment to sensuous experience) are able to see directly and to infer indirectly the Ideas through their pursuit of philosophical knowledge; in Plato's ideal republic, they rule as Philosopher-Kings.

Arguably, dualism made its first major appearance on the scene of Western thought in the form of Plato's systematic Idealism. The philosophical stage was thereby set for Aristotle, who had been Plato's student, to make the conceptual separation between the observer and the thing observed the basis for his pre-modern scientific insights, particularly in biology. That crucial dualistic distancing (even if only by a few inches) would eventually become, via the school of philosophical/religious thought called Scholasticism, the methodological centerpiece of Western science and technology — by far the most successful means ever devised to affect and control nature. The invaluable achievements of the natural sciences and the technology that is produced by and produces them have over the last 300 years lent unparalleled credibility and prestige to the scientific method, which is the synthesis of observation and "mathematicization" — the conceptual transformation of the natural universe (associated with Bacon, Galileo, and Newton), into a kind of grand mechanism whose component parts can be fully described and its movements fully predicted, at least in theory, in terms of laws, formulas, and equations. That method, closely associated with all sorts of material advantages, has allowed Western culture to dominate the world; there is virtually no place on earth, nor any aspect of human life, where Western science and technology — and the dualistic way of thinking/seeing in which they are rooted — have not penetrated and become completely identified with what "reason" itself is.

No wonder, then, that in the 19th century, when it appeared that modern science was the instrument with which "man" would ultimately subdue nature completely, the so-called social sciences — psychology, anthropology, sociology — came into existence modeled on the universalist, systematic natural sciences. Their object was to discover the "laws" which supposedly govern the movement of individuals as well as masses of human beings: the hundreds of millions of people crowding into the cities of Western Europe and the United States to work in the new factories and eventually to buy (back) what they themselves produced, and the hundreds of millions of people in Asia, Africa, and Latin America who would extract (their own — or nature's) raw materials to be manufactured. Throughout the 19th century and the first half of the 20th, any approach which deviated from the scientific method and the epistemological model that combined observation and the derivation of patterns based on mathematical or quasi-mathematical measurements would have been almost unthinkable.

All this is to say that dualism is a social invention — one which has been extraordinarily useful to human beings, and under whose total domination we have lived for the last few hundred (some might argue few thousand) years. Now, however, dualism — this vastly powerful perspective/method/model/insight — and its consequences are being challenged on the grounds that they may well have outlived their usefulness. The prospect is overwhelming. What for centuries was the principal force driving human development forward is being seen by more and more people (including me) as an impediment to further human development. Now the question is: How are we to overthrow this once highly useful and still enormously powerful assumption?

The challenge to dualism

Despite the dominance of dualism, dissent from it is not new. From the vantage point of non-Western philosophies and religions (those of the indigenous peoples of Asia and the Pacific Islands, Africa, and the Americas), most of which are monistic belief systems predating the Greeks and dualism, the notion that human life can be understood in reductionistic either/or (law of the excluded middle) terms is seen as childishly simplistic and naive. At worst it is a dangerously arrogant form of blasphemy, neither God nor Nature being subject to the laws of logic. However, the successes attributable to the scientific paradigm — and the economic and political domination of the West/North with which it has been associated over the centuries — relegated such critiques beyond the pale of what is deemed serious, reasonable thought. After all, the West has defined reason itself.

Meditation, yoga and acupuncture, for example, are frequently effective alternatives to Western medicine. Yet the philosophical perspectives from which they're derived simply haven't accomplished a great deal, pragmatically speaking. They may be morally superior. They may be spiritually enlightening. They may be aesthetically advanced. But they haven't produced anything that can compete with Western science and technology — especially as judged by Western criteria! And so the Asian/African/Amerindian insistence on seamlessness and unity, however poetic and profound those ideas may be, carries little social weight or influence.

The same may be said of the dissent from dualism, humanist and otherwise, within Western culture itself. "Unscientific" has evolved into an accusation almost equivalent in force to the term "heretic" of the Middle Ages, hurled at anyone and everyone whose thinking does not conform to the tenets of Science (the modern incarnation of Reason).

The following anecdote illustrates rather nicely how Science has come to be religiosified. Not long ago my very dear friend, Dr. Lois Holzman, spent a week training students from Eureka Free University in Moscow. An independent teacher training college whose curriculum and teaching methods have been influenced by the work of Lev Vygotsky, Eureka had invited Lois — one of the world's leading Vygotskian scholars — and another American, along with several Vygotsky experts from Russia, to be guest lecturers at its annual summer session (which was being held in London). All of the lecturers and the students met every evening to discuss the work they had done in their various classes earlier in the day.

On the second evening of the session, Lois reported that she and her students hadn't been able to build much together that day because they were too busy trying to understand each other. (She does not speak Russian and most of them don't speak English.)

"You can't build anything unless you understand what you're building," one of the Russian lecturers responded, kindly. Lois reminded him of Vygotsky's view that understanding does not precede creative activity but comes *with* it.

"Only God can create without understanding what he is creating," said the Vygotsky expert.

"Then maybe human beings need to imitate God," Lois suggested.

"God doesn't allow that!" objected the Russian, scandalized.

I don't presume to know what God does and does not allow. What *is* certain, however, is that the official spokesmen for Science, and Reason, don't allow it.

In recent years (since the collapse of Soviet communism has rendered the label "red" increasingly obsolete), the term "cult" has taken over as a means of stigmatizing those who do not think within the prevailing dualistic paradigm which is the basis not only of Science but of the established religions and orthodox (in America) two-party politics. Regardless of *what* they may think, the scientifically/politically/religiously unorthodox (like "primitive" people elsewhere in the world) are dismissed as irrational, superstitious, and ignorant; their leaders are denounced as charlatans who exploit others' credulity for their own aggrandizement.

Proponents of alternative practices and beliefs might

argue — rightly, in my opinion — that they have not in fact
sought to compete with Science; competitiveness is not so easily reconcilable with a monistic, relation-based (as opposed to
an identity-based) perspective. That they have chosen not to
do battle, however, hasn't prevented the standard-bearers of
dualism from conquering the world with it. And regardless of
what anyone may think or feel about their victory, the fact
remains that the criteria for what constitutes successful understanding have become entirely identified with the dualistic
paradigm. Like it or not, everywhere in the world all other
modes of understanding are held up for comparison with a
science that has brought electricity, running water, antibiotics,
and the shortwave radio to hundreds of millions of human
beings who otherwise would still be living much as our Iron
Age ancestors did.

This is not to say that the masses of the world's people
necessarily feel any self-conscious reverence for or allegiance
to the scientific method and the values connected with the
assumption of dualism as such. There has been no campaign
to win over the minds and hearts of the have-nots to an appreciation of Science, as there was a massive and highly successful public relations effort in the first half of this century to
persuade the American people that "progress is our most
important product" (the advertising slogan of the General
Electric corporation during the '50s). In these postmodern
times technology appears as a disembodied thing in itself,
completely detached from its origins in the scientific pursuit of
modern ideals such as Progress. Quite understandably, the billions of people in Asia, Africa, and Latin America who live at
the margins of subsistence are not terribly interested in the
philosophical question of whether the lights, the water, the
medicine, the radio, represent Progress. They simply and quite

justifiably want them! It is not surprising, then, that no critical theory challenging Science — not to mention dualism — will be produced at the periphery or the semi-periphery of Western culture, where the benefits of modern technology are no less remote than Platonic ideals.

The most passionate critiques of the scientific method, and hence of dualism itself, have come from within the Western cultural tradition. They have taken a variety of forms, from the dialectical materialism of Karl Marx (throughout most of this century and the last it was the only rigorous and systematic monistic challenge to the assumption of dualism) to the current wave of popular interest in reincarnation, contemporary critical theory in Psychology, the recent proliferation of new religions, and the latest attempts by feminist scholars to redraw the terrain of intellectual inquiry.

Ironically, the debate is heating up much more now that Marxism has fallen into disrepute. For these days still-employed intellectuals can enter the fray without jeopardizing their chances of getting grants, promotions, and tenure because they are "reds." I believe that this debate over Science and Reason is ultimately much more profound — politically, economically, morally, culturally, and socially — than the one between "capitalism" and "communism," which events of the last few years have rendered irrelevant. In my view, the challenge to dualism as manifest in the scientific paradigm is the challenge of our lifetime.

The most telling argument against dualism, in my opinion, rests on the fact that modern science — having reached its zenith in the late 1930s and early '40s (with the astounding feat that was the discovery of nuclear energy) — has at last come up against the limits of its own method. This is the same method that produced the extraordinary achievements which for the last 300 years have been used to prove dualism's validity, as well as to justify the right to rule of those who were "wise" enough to have acquired political ownership of the ideology and technology to which the scientific paradigm gave birth.

Even while dualism was becoming established as the dominant philosophical worldview, and the bipartisan American heirs to Plato's Philosopher-Kings were consolidating their political power as the leaders of the "free world" in opposition to the Soviet "anti-Christ," advances in the physical sciences themselves during the first part of this century — Gödel's discoveries in the foundations of mathematics; the work of Wittgenstein and his mentor, Bertrand Russell, also in the foundations of mathematics; Planck's discoveries in physics; Heisenberg's in quantum physics; and Einstein's seminal theory of relativity — were already revealing methodological fault lines in the bedrock of Western thought. However, these theoretical breakthroughs were being made at a moment when modern science, through technology, still held out the promise that the back-breaking labor and material deprivation which had characterized human existence throughout the millennia would soon be made obsolete; hundreds of millions of ordinary people in the United States and Western Europe were about to gain access to a standard of living that even emperors of earlier times could hardly have imagined. The critical geniuses might come up with whatever challenges to it they liked; Science, the institution, was above reproach.

However, the most recent anti-scientific discoveries in the sciences have made the cracks in the dominant paradigm increasingly visible. They come at a time when there is very widespread and profound dissatisfaction with professional politicians and the corporate interests they are seen to favor

— many of which are directly connected to a science and technology that seem far more committed to political profiteering than to progress. Moreover, these discoveries have become the subject of a more or less public dialogue conducted by social scientists and humanist scholars whose credentials and positions at or close to the apex of the academic hierarchy make them nearly (although not completely) immune to charges that they are merely crackpots, sore losers, or worse. (During his lifetime Michel Foucault, the dissident French psychologist and philosopher whose brilliantly argued and erudite polemics against modern science attracted a huge and ardent following, was routinely disparaged by the scientific orthodoxy as a cult leader; since his death in 1984 he has been officially "rehabilitated.")

It is being suggested, for example, that there may be limits to what is knowable — a suggestion that would have seemed practically obscene throughout the 19th century and most of the 20th. For it has long been a central canon of the scientific belief system that eventually Science would yield (at least in principle) a correct characterization of the universe, its movement, and everything it contains. This happy ending for human comprehension was viewed as being just a matter of time; sooner or later, the scientists self-servingly predicted, they would sufficiently refine their theory and their instruments so as to make them capable of explaining it all and, in doing so, produce a solution (or at least a possible solution) to every problem.

Today, in the opinion of many people, such optimism (or self-congratulation) appears not to have much of a foundation. There is a growing acknowledgment that the world may in fact not be fully knowable by the human mind — which is, after all, just one element of the world that scientists used to think could and eventually would be known in its entirety. Contemporary discoveries in physics, mathematics, methodology, and other fields reveal that much of what goes on just doesn't seem to fit the logical patterns Western science has traditionally found to comprehend it. What if those patterns are wrong? What if there are logical patterns yet to be found? What if some, or most, of "reality" is unpatterned? The dualistic scientific paradigm may still be the most effective means of knowing what is knowable. But what if there simply are no logical patterns to be found for everything, however long science may search and however powerful its instruments? What if some things simply can't be known?

Not long ago, the *New York Times* reported in its weekly "Science Times" section the belief of Dr. James Hartle, a distinguished cosmologist at the University of California at Santa Barbara, that "the notion of separate laws that exist independent of the lawmakers might have to be jettisoned as so much 'excess baggage.' We can't stand separate from creation and view it as though it were one of our computer simulations." In other words, Professor Hartle was questioning the assumption of dualism!

He is not alone. At the prestigious Santa Fe Institute in New Mexico, some of the most highly regarded (and straitlaced) scientists in the world have been asking quasi-postmodern philosophical questions like: "Is the real world too complex for our limited minds?" "Are there important problems that lie forever beyond our reach?" "Must we consider casting aside the problem-solution epistemological model?"

In asking such questions these scientists would seem, at first glance, to be daring to challenge the whole scientific kit and caboodle. However, a closer look often reveals that they are actually making a sophisticated attempt to marshal evidence in its favor by conducting rigorous studies of phenomena which appear not to be governed by any patterns or laws and in doing so to bring whatever is presently not explained in from the cold of the unknowable, the unpredictable, the emergent. They are in many cases merely seeking to transform logic in such a way as to enable it to take into account those things for which there is presently no accounting, to come up with what might be called a logic of the illogical, lawful methods for understanding unlawful processes, a paradigmatic analysis of emergent (non-paradigmatic) phenomena and processes — all this despite the fact that such phenomena and processes apparently insist on ignoring not only the existing laws and paradigms but legislation and paradigmization. Sometimes they sound a bit like the family of an ax murderer clinging to the pretense that their relative may misbehave himself every now and then, but he's really an ordinary guy — you just have to get to know him.

Science defends itself

The fact that a well organized and sustained critique of Science (however "friendly") is emanating from the citadels of Western/Northern European thought itself is creating something that looks very much like panic among members of the academic scientific establishment. Not long ago, 200 of them held a three-day meeting in New York City to decry "the flight from science and reason." (The story was covered by both the *New York Times* and the *Wall Street Journal*.) For if this flight should become a mass movement, the modernists are likely to forfeit not only their status and their tenure but the highly lucrative grants that are their lifeblood. So, waving the banner of Reason, the grant-ocracy sallied forth to defend Science — in the course of which defense they issued a warning, intended for their political patrons, that the assault on Reason (dualism) threatens to destroy Democracy (two-partyism). "Fortunately," the *Wall Street Journal* editorialized, "some are beginning to realize that 'anti-science' is a serious threat that calls for an active defense."

Revealingly, the conference was at least as anti-scientific as any of the targets which the participants lumped together and attacked broadside: faith healing; astrology; religious fundamentalism; the actress and spiritualist Shirley MacLaine; the various social constructionists; and the postmodern critics within their own ranks, who were accused of distorting the work of Einstein, Planck and others to prove the heresy that science is not the source of universal truth but merely a particular system of values and beliefs. No scientific analysis was offered by the scientists to explain why Science is coming under such intense critical scrutiny these days, why some of the best scientific scholars are participating in the charge, or why critiques originating from very different sources — mainstream and "fringe," scholarly and popular, "right" and "left," religious and political — appear to be converging. No effort was made to ensure scientific objectivity; opposing views were neither invited nor welcomed.

A defense of Science and Reason! Such a thing would have seemed preposterous and absurd even a relatively short time ago. For three centuries, it went without saying that the scientific paradigm, the scientific method, was correct. Now that's becoming somewhat less than obvious.

Science, supposedly the highest form of Reason, started out — politically speaking — as a radical critique of the existing power arrangements between church and state; you may remember that Galileo was excommunicated for saying that the sun did not revolve around the Earth. Three hundred fifty years later, Science — long entrenched in a marriage of considerable convenience to the secular state — seems more and more to be abandoning the premises and principles that guided its early attempts to understand the natural universe in favor of a crudely self-serving pragmatism: "The moral authority of science depends on maintaining a good sense of self, and recognizing the need to act in self-protection," Dr. Gerald Horton, a professor of physics at Harvard University, told his colleagues at the flight-from-reason conference in New York City. A physicist, invoking the jargon of pop psychology in the name of Science! Nothing, in my opinion, could point more forcefully to the need for a historical, tool-and-result, assumption-free method than this anachronistic insistence on the right of the societally identified knowers (the Scientist-Kings) to rule forever.

What's wrong with this picture?

Dualism won the day because on the basis of it Science and Reason were able to produce the solution — a very brilliant solution — to a problem that had been engaged in the West for a thousand years or more: How can human beings comprehend the workings of nature so as to master it? The invention of dualism-in-the-form-of-science ended the millennium-long search for a method that would allow "man" to assert his superiority over the rest of "nature" (which, as a number of feminist scholars have pointed out, was identified as female). As such, dualistic science was enormously, indisputably successful. The distancing of the observer from the observed — the essential attitude of dualism — and the derivation of formulas, patterns and laws (expressed in mathematical terms) from such observation are precisely suited to the study of physical phenomena, whether far-off stars or nearby microbes. In my opinion the success of Science can be attributed in large part to the coherence, accidental or otherwise, between its method (the *how* of its knowing) and its object (the *what* is to be known).

It doesn't follow, however, that a human science using that same method would be similarly successful; on the contrary. For human beings possess characteristics that are not only not natural but "anti-natural." These characteristics happen not to be incidental to our species; they are the very ones that distinguish us from the rest of nature. We engage in the self-conscious, ongoing historical activity of creating culture, which in turn determines who and how we are; our nature is, fundamentally, at once *both* socially constructed *and* emergent (that is, not fixed). A "science" that does not take these facts of human life into account is therefore a contradiction in terms.

In studying human beings through the lens of dualism, psychologists confront an insuperable and obvious methodological difficulty: human life activity is not separable from the life activity of the psychologists themselves. That is, the scientist — unlike the distant star or the nearby microbe — is both the observer and the observed. By forcing the assumption of dualism (objectivity) on that unity, psychologists produce a distorted picture, a misrepresentation, of it; this distortion is what I mean by the myth of Psychology. Self-referentiality (our capacity to refer to ourselves) and the paradoxes associated with it are not trivial but fundamental features of human existence.

Historical activity: The alternative to knowing

In social therapy, we are not concerned to come up with a truer picture, a better representation, a more lucid explanation, a sharper interpretation, a superior myth. Rather, we are engaged in the practical-critical, ongoing historical activity of creating culture — an alternative to reified and alienated pictures, representations, explanations, interpretations, myths.

That is, social therapy is an anti-explanatory approach to human understanding and human development. For not only is there a great deal that is emergent within human psychological life, in my opinion so much is emergent — life is so completely and fundamentally self-reflexive and self-referential — that the very model of understanding which has held sway for the last several hundred years has to be challenged if we are to understand ourselves/develop at all.

No matter how hard we may push, squeeze, cut, stretch, categorize, describe, and otherwise manipulate human life activity, it simply cannot be made to fit into the traditional Western scientific "objective" model that has been put to such effective use since the 17th century for comprehending nature. The point is not that there are dimensions of human life which are aberrant or emergent (as in "abnormal psychology"); it is that human life as a totality is so essentially non-patternized activity that any attempt to patternize or objectify it is necessarily a distortion of it.

This is not to say that life, which I take to be fundamentally non-explainable, cannot be explained. After all, it's possible to apply paint to the ocean — not the most sensible thing to be doing, perhaps, but certainly possible. Similarly, it is possible to apply explanations to human life activity which are well-formed, cogent, and comprehensible in an abstract, static, pictorial sense but that nevertheless cannot be used for development.

This raises a very interesting question about the relationship between what is logically possible and what is developmental. For it turns out that they are not at all the same thing. The most recent edition of the *Diagnostic and Statistical Manual (DSM-IV)* published by the American Psychiatric Association, for example, is a massive catalogue of mental and emotional diseases, all named, described and explained in the best (that is, worst) scientific tradition of taxonomy. It is certainly possible to superimpose the theoretical construct of Attention Deficit Disorder on a seven-year-old — the life of that child can be made to fit the picture — but what if the picture is...just a picture? Once the diagnosis is made, *where is there room for development?*

Contemporary medicine has come up with all sorts of explanations and accountings for physical illness which may be completely logical from the perspective of the traditional scientific paradigm; the thing has a name, it belongs to a category of illnesses, it can be explained in terms of known causes, this is the treatment, these are the side effects, that is the prognosis. Yet such explanations, descriptions, and accountings are often so abstract as to make no sense, to be of no practical relevance whatsoever, to the patient who is ostensibly being treated. Indeed, they frequently are substituted for the patient.

Now some people might argue that patients don't need their treatment to make sense to them; it might even be argued that it's preferable for patients to be "out of it." Perhaps when it comes to surgery, for example, what's most desirable is for the patient to lie there, unconscious, while the experts operate, and to wake up only when it's all over.

But what about all those situations that call for the active participation of the human being who happens to be a patient — human situations that, if they are not to be dehumanizing and inhumane, necessarily involve growth, development, transformation? (I'll have more to say in Section III about how patients need to participate with their doctors in the joint activity of building a zone of proximal development where they are supported to create/perform their physical health.) What if the seemingly infinite descriptions, categories, explanations, accountings, and interpretations — the "knowing" — of human life that Science and the "social" (pseudo-)sciences are able to come up with are inconsistent with the continued *development* of our life, as individuals and as a species? What if Science is actually holding back the growth of our physical, emotional, social, and moral being? What if the epoch of transformation through Science is over? And what if Science itself is incapable of answering such questions?

LET'S PERFORM!

Many of us have a favorite performer, someone we think is the greatest. Our hero or heroine may be an actor or an actress, a singer or a musician, or perhaps an athlete. We try to see them whenever they're playing, live, or on TV; we follow their careers; we know their life stories; we appreciate their creativity. And most of us assume that what they do when they're up there on the screen or the stage, or out there on the court or the field — performing — is an activity which we — ordinary people — don't, can't, maybe even shouldn't, do in everyday life except in special circumstances. Professional performers themselves are likely to share that assumption; they stop performing, or believe that they ought to, the moment the curtain comes down or the game ends (the moment they stop getting paid to do it).

It's true that ordinary people don't, or at least tend not to, perform except in those special circumstances. But even if people believe that they have no talent (in other words, that they wouldn't be any good at performing), it's unlikely that they don't perform because they simply can't *possibly* do it. For performing is how all of us, as young children, first learn not only to speak but to do everything else that enables us to participate in societal life — to become part of our common culture. *But that's different!* you may object. *After all, we do all kinds of things as children — like crawling under a gate or hiding in a small space — that we're unable to do later on.* Obviously, that's true.

The point I'm trying to make here, however, is not that as adults we can continue to do the "what" of a particular childhood performance. Rather it's that performance, going beyond ourselves, the strange activity of being who we aren't — whoever that may be at any given moment — is, as I tried to show earlier, essential to our human-ness. To refrain from performing, therefore, is not at all the same thing as to "stop behaving like a child." It is, in my opinion, to deny our uniquely human capacity to choose who and how we are to be. Which is why I believe that *shouldn't* perform is one of the more destructive, status quo-serving rules of societal ethics ever invented. For in the absence of performing, we have no means of going beyond the role determined behavior called for by the institutions of society.

This is not to say that behavior, rules, and roles are problematic by definition. On the contrary, they produce the societal stability which makes our day to day, collective life possible. In referring to things by name, telling time, buying and selling, asking questions to get answers, opening bank accounts, and shutting doors (along with the infinite variety of other acts which are regarded as normal behavior), we are unquestioningly accepting the cultural assumptions that determine how we are, and how we see. If we were to abandon behavior entirely in favor of the constant creation of new ways of being and seeing, the living of everyday life would be practically impossible.

Yet to engage exclusively in behavior, as many adults do, day in and day out, year in and year out, is to be deprived of the exhilaration and freedom of performing, the expression of our equally necessary and equally natural historical creativity. All too many people, transfixed by the illusory appearances which they see in the societal mirrors, are tragically unaware that they themselves (as members of a family, an ethnic group, a nation, our species) are the historical creators of those marvelous societal illusions.

In my view, the rule that no one except a professional has any business performing effectively denies us the possibility of a joyous life. The exclusion of ordinary people from performatory activity prevents us from comprehending the unique paradox which is human nature — the fact that we, unlike any other species, are both quantitatively (societally) determined and qualitatively (historically) free. And it's only in embracing that paradox, philosophically and performatorily, that we can discover joy.

The essence of performance is collective, social, joint, creative imitation. That is, it is something which human beings with various levels of experience and expertise (like little Jennie and her Mommy) do together in such a way as to produce something new from whatever cultural materials may be at hand. In its purest form, performance is a historical activity that has no purpose, point, use, or meaning. Performance is very much like some poems which — unlike newspaper articles, religious sermons, drivers' manuals, political speeches, mystery novels, cookbooks, scholarly essays, and most ordinary conversation — often have no purpose or use. These poems do not "stand for" anything other than themselves; as the poet Archibald MacLeish once put it, "a poem should not mean, but be."

Think of very young children, like Jennie, who have not yet acquired self-consciousness, performing in the zpd. In playing language games with more experienced speakers, they are performing poetically; they imitate the sounds they hear without any notion of "communicating," without any regard for the rules that govern language, without any degree of awareness that this thing they are doing can be used for, or mean, anything.

Remember that imitation is not to be confused with mimicry, the entirely purposeful attempt to reproduce as closely as possible the thing being mimicked. Actors whose skill lies in impersonating well known personalities, forgers, plagiarists, and amateur "copycats" are all engaged in mimicry. Unlike imitation, which is thoroughly social, mimicry doesn't require the participation of another human being. In fact, mimicry is not exclusive to human beings; among some kinds of monkeys, parrots, insects, and even plants, it's relatively common behavior.

Imitation, which I am suggesting only human beings do, is the building upon and transformation — the completing — of what is already there in such a way as to make it anew; that is, our labor creates more value than the work that went into it. Imitation is rooted in our capacity for collective self-consciousness, the unique (yet often forgotten) ability that human beings have to view our own social activity even as we are engaging in it. This is not the same as saying that there's nothing new under the sun; the remarkable thing is that we are constantly creating something new (going beyond ourselves) from what is already there. It is through this creative process that human beings, unlike any other species, continuously produce culture — which, in turn, produces us. Human creativity, "added" to what's already there, produces something which is not only more, but other, than what there was.

I am referring here not to culture in the narrowest sense, as a synonym for art ("high culture") or entertainment ("popular culture"). Nor am I referring to culture in the anthropological sense, to describe the set of customs, beliefs, and artifacts that characterize the lifestyle of a particular group of people ("Amish culture" or "the drug culture"). Culture, as I am using it here, includes art and entertainment — along with the high/low, good/bad dualistic paradigm, or way of seeing, that distinguishes between them. Culture in the broadest sense also embraces customs, beliefs and artifacts — as well as how it is that people comprehend these products of their collective creation, the process that produces them, and themselves as producers. In other words, what I mean by culture is the complex, socially constructed array of assumptions, explanations, stories, and accountings with which people view/make sense of the world and the life that they create.

In our Western (dualistic) culture we tend to make a sharp distinction between "the real thing" and what is "merely" imitation. The fact is, however, that all of human culture is the product of collective, self-conscious, creative imitation; as a species, we are constantly completing ourselves and our lives — not finishing, but transforming in a way that takes further what has already been made in an ongoing developmental process that has no end/point. This creative human activity that characterizes all cultural production, but which in our culture is frequently hidden from view, is often most visible in the arts.

Take jazz, for example. The legendary Louis Armstrong started out his career in the early 1920s playing trumpet in a band led by Joseph "King" Oliver, himself a tremendously talented jazz trumpeter. The young "Satchmo" completed the

King — not by "finishing" what Oliver had "started" but by imitating the older man's music in such a way as to transform it into something new: swing. The swing era produced the trumpeter Roy Eldridge, who imitated and transformed Armstrong's innovations; in the '40s, his music was in turn imitated — and transformed — by the big band trumpeter Dizzy Gillespie. With the tenor saxophonist Charlie Parker, Gillespie was the inventor of be-bop — a whole new way of playing music that became the foundation of modern jazz. Since then, two successive generations of trumpeters, including Miles Davis and Wynton Marsalis, have been imitating and building on Gillespie's innovations.

Gifted as these men were/are, they did not bring jazz into the world singlehandedly (or even together); rather, they all (including the ones who are no longer physically alive) participate in a "zone of musical development" with other musicians, and with the millions of people who listen to jazz. Over a period of 70 years or more, this ensemble of human beings has collectively created a way of playing/hearing sounds that is simultaneously as old as the first musical instrument and as new as the improvisation you may have heard last night on Basin Street in New Orleans or at the Blue Note in New York City's Greenwich Village. And the creative beat goes on…

This is how all of human culture (not just Culture with a capital "C") develops. Every new human-made thing in the world is created through the ongoing, social process of imitation. What is perhaps most remarkable of all is that every human being participates in this process, at least in the first few years of life. For it is through performance — the ongoing historical activity of creative imitation which produces culture — that children become acculturated/adapted to society.

Picture Jennie as a new baby (a born performer). She lies in her crib, sleeping much of the time. When she's awake, other people — typically Mommy, occasionally Daddy, Grandma, perhaps her teenage cousin or a baby sitter — feed and bathe her, change her diapers, pick her up, play peek-a-boo and other games with her. They also continue going about the business of their lives in her presence, without necessarily paying attention to her; she's there, and simply as a consequence of that fact she's included in their ongoing collective life. At this very early moment, Jennie is in some ways not much different from the plants on the window sill or Tip, the pet turtle, whose home is a glass tank in the living room; she is, like them, an organism that requires care and reacts to stimuli.

But of course she is also entirely different from the plants and from Tip. As a human being among other human beings, Jennie will become not merely more of who she already is (taller, heavier, stronger, bigger), but someone other than who she is; that is, she has the capacity — as these other living things do not — for unlimited (cultural) development and growth.

One of the (cultural) things those other human beings around her are doing is talking. They talk to each other and — surprisingly — they sometimes talk to Jennie. It's surprising because Jennie hasn't any inkling of what they're talking about! Nor does she know that in making the sounds they make, they're doing something called "talking." And while Jennie doesn't know this (for in fact she doesn't know much of anything), they nevertheless relate to her as a language speaker. How? By playing language games with her. Why? Simply because she's there and, unlike the plants and the turtle, she is "one of us."

Although she doesn't know very much, Jennie possesses the physical ability to make sounds. And she does. (Even babies who are deaf do so.) Very soon Jennie begins to mimic, more or less at random, what she hears, narrowing the range of the sounds she makes to whatever is "in the air." At first Jennie mimics just as parrots do, seemingly without rhyme or reason. Italian, Japanese, Xhosa, Urdu, Texan twang or New Yorkese — they're all the same to babies, who reproduce the sounds made by the people around them without any regard for their meaning or use and oblivious of the fact that there are such things as meaning and use. Indeed, babies are oblivious of most things: that there are facts, that there are sounds — and, for that matter, that there's obliviousness.

Remarkably soon, however, Jennie begins to engage in creative imitation — performance. She does this not because she thinks she can or should, or because she decides or chooses or desires to do so. Is she driven by an innate instinct? Even if she were it would not be relevant if the other human beings around her did not relate to her socially, as they do. Imitation is not fundamentally a psychological, or a biological, imperative. Rather, it is a fact of our social cultural life; it's what human beings do together. Babies who've been on the societal scene for just a short while are already imitating the more experienced speakers around them, just as the young Louis Armstrong imitated King Oliver. The difference is that babies imitate without the self-consciousness which typically both enriches and inhibits adult creativity. (Picasso once remarked that as a child he could draw like Raphael, but it had taken him a lifetime to learn to draw like children do.)

"Ba-yaba-bo-ba," says two-month-old Jennie from her perch in the baby carrier on Daddy's shoulders. It's Saturday morning, and they are at the post office buying stamps. Actually, Jennie doesn't even say things so much as she burbles, gurgles, drools, splutters and spits out noises — to which

Daddy responds with words, making a conversation with this very inexperienced speaker.

"Yes, we do have a lot of letters to mail today," he tells her, perhaps glancing around self-consciously to see if anyone is listening to this peculiar dialogue.

"Boo-aaa-blh-yo," says Jennie, performing speaking. A brand new member of the culture, she doesn't know how to do it or even what it is. Unself-conscious, it does not occur to her that she might be talking too loud or mispronouncing a word. She performs freely (purely) in history; as yet there is no self-identity to see, and — which amounts to the same thing — no self-image to be seen, in the (Jennie's) societal mirrors. The joy that adults (by performing philosophizing) may eventually come to discover in the self-conscious comprehension of their historicalness cannot be a part of Jennie's experience at this moment. Nor need it be. Performing her life, very young Jennie is unlikely to experience herself doing so. There is no self-identity/"I" to remark on or perceive "my" performance; there is only performance, "pure" performance, without a purpose or point. Nor does Jennie know anything of use or meaning; there is only the historical unself-conscious playing of language games, "pure" language activity, ungoverned by rules.

"Here's a letter to Grandma," Daddy says to Jennie, holding an envelope up. "I bet Mommy wrote her all about what you've been up to lately!"

"Ah-ya-obhl-ao," says Jennie, gazing intently at a baby in a stroller just ahead of them.

Such "conversations" go on for months between Jennie and other, more experienced speakers — Mommy, Daddy, Grandma, the four-year-old next door, the cashier at the supermarket, and everyone else in Jennie's not-so-small world. In these early language games, Jennie is performing as who she isn't, a speaker, by imitating speaking, and the other performers — for this is no one-baby show, but an ensemble performance — are responding to what Jennie is doing by talking back to her. They relate to her as a speaker long before she says her first word, supporting her to do what she doesn't know how to do — to be who she isn't. Jennie is engaged in the performatory learning that leads development which characterizes the zone of proximal development, the activity of language acquisition. She doesn't know there's anything to know; she's delightfully untroubled by any concern that she might make a mistake, look foolish, talk too much, or have nothing to say. Remember, she isn't herself yet!

Years later, Jennie is likely to find herself in a classroom where a teacher is explaining that "Mommy," "Daddy," and "Grandma" belong to a category of words called "nouns," that all words belong to one or another such category, and that there are elaborate rules of grammar which govern how they are used. The subtext of the grammar lesson will include information about the value that is placed on knowing such rules. If you obey them, you'll be identified as smart and rewarded accordingly; if not, you'll be punished with bad grades and the many negative consequences that follow. An older Jennie may be interested in all of this information (if she's concerned with how well she does on tests), or not; she hasn't needed to know it to become an increasingly skilled user of the English language.

In another classroom, she may find herself listening to another teacher explaining the rules of French grammar and assigning the students lists of French words to be memorized. That may be of some help to Jennie and the other students who are being taught to speak French. But as almost anyone who's ever tried to learn a second language in this way is likely to tell you, it's a rather tedious process with a great deal of sheer drudgery to it. Such information-acquiring, skill-getting behavior has little to do with how we as human beings come to take our places within the community of speakers of our native language, which is not a matter of knowing the societal rules beforehand but of participating with other human beings in an ensemble performance of speaking.

Imitating the people around her, little Jennie comes to see that when she makes particular sounds they are responded to in particular ways. Now the meanings of words, defined by the social context long before she knows their dictionary definition, enter the picture. In learning the meanings of words, Jennie is simultaneously learning to use — and to identify herself as a user — of them. There comes that most extraordinary and completely ordinary day when Jennie, not yet a year old, first says: "Ma-ma." These are not just any sounds, nor is this an arbitrary activity. They are particular sounds, forming a particular utterance. Jennie has spoken her first *word*, a sound with meaning, uttered for a use; perhaps she is trying to get her mother's attention.

It is in this most extraordinary, completely ordinary historical moment that Jennie first experiences self-consciousness. For the first time she has participated, and been aware that she was participating, in the cultural practice of language-using, putting sounds together in an *If-I-make-this-sound-she'll-stop-whatever-she's-doing-and-respond-to-me* sort of way. Having begun to be aware that she possesses the quite amazing ability to produce sounds, Jennie rapidly learns to exercise that ability self-consciously — for a purpose, with a use.

In the same way, she's becoming aware that she can do all sorts of other things she's been doing without being aware that she could, or even that there was an "I" to do them — opening and closing her eyes, moving her fingers and toes, turning her head to look in the direction of a noise, smiling...Her sense of her self emerges from her increasingly self-conscious participation in the social ensemble; she becomes capable of observing: *I can do this!* This is how we each acquire a self-identity, a privatized and individuated self which has relationships with other individuated selves — *relationship* being what simultaneously reconciles and maintains the distance between self and other (meanwhile verifying the "authenticity" of this quintessential Western duality). Paradoxically, the self emerges out of a thoroughly social activity.

Already Jennie is stepping out of the realm of pure performance, the zpd where she unself-consciously played language games; she is beginning to be adapted to society. Within the next few years, Jennie will become increasingly skillful at using language to accomplish all sorts of societal ends: to express her needs and desires and opinions; to get other people to laugh, or to like her, or to listen to what she has to say; to impart and receive information...As she does so she will be less and less likely to exercise her poetic, creative capacity for making meaning. Eventually, Jennie will enter into the fully alienated self-conscious adult world of societal adaptation where performance is as "unnatural" as poetry — a world in which the prosaic, rule governed use of language unabashedly asserts its authority over the poetic unruliness of meaning-making.

One of the most remarkable things about this very remarkable process is the paradoxical fact that we become societal users of language as a consequence of our prior participation with other human beings in the historical activity of making meaning/culture. It's only by taking part in the historical and thoroughly social activity of creative imitation — performance — that we're subsequently able to adapt to the complex, rule governed societal behavior of language use.

The random, mimicking noises Jennie made at first give way to sounds that are obviously imitative and as such indicate her dawning awareness that she is making them. In learning the societal uses/meanings of language Jennie is simultaneously acquiring a consciousness of herself as a language user. That is, at some moment in this very complex cultural/social process, children become aware that they are participating in a social activity with other people. Jennie's capacity to reflect on what she is doing with Mommy and Daddy and the others (as well as *that* she is doing something with them, that there is something to be done with them, and that she is capable of doing it) is itself an element of the process which both produces self-consciousness and is further enhanced by it.

Momentarily, perhaps, Jennie is able to catch a glimpse of the historical, social process through which the fully privatized, individuated being she will eventually become is being formed — and in that very moment she becomes alienated, as possibly she will be for the rest of her life (although I hope not), from the process that made the glimpsing possible. Every human being experiences the trauma of this stunning transition, so poignant and profoundly ironic, when we see the social and in that act of seeing are compelled to be aware of the alienated self that alone sees the social.

This traumatic moment, in which the existential irony of adult human life is abruptly revealed to us, engenders a crisis that, in my opinion, only philosophizing can ultimately cure. For philosophizing is what restores some sense of history which is otherwise likely to be lost to us forever in that singularly thrilling, terrifying moment when we first encounter our selves and, in doing so, become aware (from a distance) of the historicalness that we could not have known until then.

From this moment on, children in our culture begin to be actively discouraged from performing. Picture Jennie at six years old, a creative imitator who's learned not only to speak but to read and write. She gets dressed by herself, brushes her teeth, puts away her toys, blows her nose, waits her turn, says please and thank you when she's supposed to; she feels sad when Tip the turtle dies, she looks forward to summer camp, she's embarrassed if she's scolded. By now Jennie has a whole array of adaptive societal skills, knowledge, and emotions that enable her to participate competently in the institutions of society: she goes to school, watches television, has friends.

Jennie also has a little brother, Joey, who at 18 months is the baby of the family. Jennie has a different part to play in the social ensemble now; within the zone of proximal development, *she* is one of the more experienced speakers who, along with Mommy and Daddy, is expected to complete for Joey. When she competes with him instead, they are liable to be annoyed: "Stop acting like a baby," Mommy tells her impatiently when Jennie won't let Joey play with one of her toys or spouts nonsense syllables in response to a question. "You know better than that," Daddy says disapprovingly when Jenny makes a snowman's face with the mashed potatoes and peas on her plate, or blows bubbles with her milk, at the dinner table.

The adults in her life — Mommy, Daddy, her first-grade teacher — are demanding that Jennie act her age, set an example for Joey, behave herself, know the difference between right and wrong. As official spokespersons on behalf of societal stability and the institutions which maintain it, their bias is in favor of the consistency and predictability that characterize role determined, rule governed behavior. Increasingly, Jennie's expected to be exactly (and only) the societal person she's already become: someone who's old enough to be taken to the movies, ride a bicycle, invite other children to her birthday party, and make choices about what to wear. Which means, to the adults, that she's too old to jump and tumble and fall down (except at the playground), play with imaginary friends, or engage in any of the other poetic/performatory activities that adults welcome and participate in with very young children. Yet while Jennie may no longer be an unself-conscious baby, she has not yet, perhaps, acquired the hardened self-identity of a fully self-conscious adult. At six, she's not entirely invested in societal stability; she's still capable of and drawn to performing (imitating) who she isn't. Nevertheless, as Jennie continues to adapt, the adults around her see to it that performance is resolutely shunted aside in favor of proper (rule governed) behavior except on the special occasions (Halloween, the class play) or in the special places (the baseball field, the swimming pool) when and where performing is acceptable.

Allie, the eight-year-old daughter of one of my patients, was brought up to the front of her third-grade class and ridiculed by the teacher for handing in a science report that she had written in the form of a poem. A one-of-a-kind educational "horror story"? Sadly, I don't think it is. Before they've finished elementary school, most children have stopped performing altogether; their creativity seems to have evaporated; by the time they're nine or ten they are no longer the poets they were at two and three. Instead, they are themselves!

This is how most of us lose the sense of our historicalness — the sense of how we got to where we are — while we are still children. Denied access to the performatory historical stage where human beings engage in collective, social, joint, creative imitation, we are left alone with our self-identity — alienated and well on our way to the extended existential crisis of the fully adapted adult. That momentary glimpse we had of ourselves as members of the social ensemble is largely forgotten; we become fully the images that appear in the societal mirrors, nothing else.

You can see societal behavior taking over from historical performance when children who are just beginning to learn the rules (and that there are rules) themselves become "fanatic" about them. "You can't do that!" a six-year-old is likely to tell a younger child who is making up a game of cards as they go along. "That's silly!" a five-year-old will scold an adult who puts the baby's hat on his own head for fun. "That's a girl's toy!" a four-year-old boy may object when the receptionist in the pediatrician's office hands him a teddy bear. The more adapted we become, the harder it is for us to play games (perform) in history — unless, and until, as adults we make the *choice* to perform again. We do so not as children, but as who we are: self-conscious adults. Then it's possible for us to say: "I'm breaking a rule? So what? After all, it's only a rule."

At the Off-Off-Broadway Castillo Theatre in New York City where I am the artistic director, we are creating what I call developmental theatre: a theatrical zone of proximal development where ordinary people, including the actors on the stage, the technical crew, the producer, the director, and the playwright (whether alive or dead, physically present or not) and the audience can participate together in a philosophical dialogue (performance), the subject (and form) of which is theatre.

This is not another way of saying "art for art's sake." We're not trying to come up with answers about life, or to give people insights into life. Nor are we trying to tell the audience how to go out and change the world, or even that they should. (Our theatre, and the community of which it is part, are too inextricably intertwined with the rest of the world for that dualistic notion to be relevant.) Like any other zone of proximal development, developmental theatre is a point-less, tool-and-result, performatory, practical-critical, playful historical activity.

Traditional theatre most often works by getting the audience to identify emotionally with the characters in a play — to empathize with them. Radical, or avant-garde, theatre works to achieve a rational/ideological identification between the audience and the characters by winning them over to progressive political ideas. The founding father of avant-garde theatre was the brilliant German playwright Bertolt Brecht, who died in 1956. (He is the author of *Mother Courage*, *The Caucasian Chalk Circle*, *The Good Woman of Szechuan*, and, with Kurt Weill, *The Threepenny Opera*.) Brecht believed, correctly in my opinion, that empathy helps to maintain the existing social and political arrangements; it illuminates, magnifies, and thereby lends legitimacy to who people already are and how they already see. (Empathy is similarly problematic, in my opinion, in personal life, where it serves to maintain the existing emotional arrangements; that is, empathy validates what people already feel and how they comprehend the doing of feeling.)

The work of Brecht and his followers is radically anti-empathic — but it isn't anti-identity. In my view, however, it's identity itself — not empathy as a means to it — that's problematic from the vantage point of development. As a playwright and a director (as well as a therapist), I'm not interested in identification of any sort: "bad" old identities or "good" new identities to which people are converted. I'm not seeking converts! What I *am* concerned to do is to show people the process of making theatre, and thereby to transform Theatre from a rule governed societal institution into the ongoing historical activity of performing. That is, we're creating theatre that isn't "really" Theatre in the same way that social therapy isn't "really" Clinical Psychology — which is precisely what makes it helpful to people. We're not in the illusion business.

When I directed the play *Red Channels* by the distinguished Black playwright Laurence Holder, for example, I wasn't attempting to create the illusion that Doug Miranda, the actor who portrayed W.E.B. DuBois, was really DuBois; I wanted DuBois, the great African American activist and scholar who died in 1963, to become Doug Miranda. This was not to leave DuBois out, or to romanticize (create an illusion of) Doug. It was to allow DuBois to shape Doug. Now this is not at all the "theatrely" thing to do; people ask: "Why should I come to see this guy Doug?" (Interestingly, the same people who are opposed to performance in "real life" on the grounds that it's "phony" are likely to insist that *only* "phoniness" counts as "real" theatre.)

My answer: Because you *are* seeing Doug! DuBois is dead, remember. Doug Miranda is quite alive! Yes, Doug is playing the DuBois character — but why does that mean we should judge how well he does by how well he does DuBois? Why shouldn't we judge DuBois by how well he shapes Doug Miranda? That's a better measure, in my view, of DuBois' current (and lasting) value. DuBois had his day, and his life. He had his hearing. Now let him help Doug Miranda to speak. That's what will allow not only the living Doug, but the dead DuBois, to go on developing. Doug imitates DuBois to create a more developed Doug.

Our culture has produced elaborate rationalizations to justify the exclusion of performance from everyday life. These justifications are reflected in the frequently heard judgment that performance is artificial, or phony, and in the aversion many people express toward imitation: *If I imitate someone else*, they worry, *my self will disappear.*

The significant difference between performance and behavior, however, is not that one is artificial and the other is natural. Rather, it's that as adults our behavior is societally determined, while adult performance requires that we self-consciously create who and how to be — who and how we aren't.

Carolyn, the assistant to the president of a publishing company, has been coming to see plays at Castillo for years. This season she volunteered to perform in a staged reading of a play that we produced as part of our annual series of "New Plays for New Days" (mostly works-in-progress by inexperienced playwrights who welcome the opportunity to show and discuss their work). Carolyn, a warm-hearted, soft-spoken woman in her late twenties who's engaged to be married, was cast in the role of a wife who blames her husband for the death of their child many years earlier; night after night, she rages at him — although the husband himself died long ago. Carolyn told me that when she first read the script she had worried: "I'll never be able to do this." Over the next few weeks she thought a lot about her character, Mary, "so angry and crazy with grief," and about women she knows — the sister of her future mother-in-law, and a cleaning lady in Carolyn's office building — who reminded her of Mary. Then came the rehearsal and, as Carolyn described it, "Things poured out of my mouth that I didn't know were inside me." They weren't, of course; they were created in the social activity of performing.

Professional actors and actresses have this experience all the time. Carolyn — like little Jennie and Louis Armstrong — actually became *more* herself in the activity of creative imitation. For in contrast to the prescribed, unself-conscious behavior that's required for the proper acting out of societal roles, performance allows us to discover/create dimensions of ourselves that we might not have known were there — or that weren't there — simply because they're not called for in the societal script. For when we perform, we draw upon experiences, attitudes and feelings that don't ordinarily find expression in the roles we're used to playing.

Carolyn wasn't less herself when she imitated a deeply embittered old woman; she was Carolyn "plus" the character of Mary she performed. Imitation doesn't diminish us; on the contrary, it pushes us beyond what we already do, feel, and perceive to be (in quantitative terms) *more* of who we already are.

But that's not the most important point. What emerges through performance is a *qualitative* transformation: in performing we re-create ourselves, becoming enhanced, enriched, developed — *other* than who we are. This is the uniquely human activity in which, as individuals and as a species, we participate in making culture, including our own "nature" — who we are, and how we see ourselves.

As a theatre director, I have found that the best actors are the ones who come to a play prepared to reassess their initial impressions of the characters they're playing; they're willing to take risks by trying new things with the material provided by the script. That is, they're not simply there to obey the playwright, the director, or the rules they learned in drama school (or picked up at the movies); they're open to using the characters as written in the script and as performed in previous productions to reach parts of themselves that they've never touched before. And that creative process doesn't stop with the final rehearsal. A talented actor, in my view, is one who continuously creates and re-creates himself or herself — from opening night to the closing performance of the play. Such

actors don't just act; they *perform*.
And that's how it is in everyday life as well.

Evelyn is a 29-year-old single mother who's recently come into social therapy because she had begun to be abusive to her seven-year-old daughter Bonny. "When I yell at her I sound just like my mother used to, and I hate myself for doing that to her. I love her more than anything," Evelyn told the group. "And I've hit her twice in the last month. I felt sick about it afterward. But I'm scared it's going to happen again. I get so angry sometimes that I feel out of control."

That's when Evelyn needs to be able to philosophize. "I don't think you get the picture," Evelyn tells me when I suggest this to her. "When I get into one of these states, it's like I've lost my mind. I'm not thinking clearly. I'm feeling frustrated, exhausted, trapped, and stupid. Philosophizing isn't in it! All I can do is express my anger and rage."

Precisely. For it's just at those moments when we can't see anything other than expressing our selves as reflected in the societal mirrors that we need to perform beyond our selves — to be who we aren't — by stepping back into history. The way to go is by philosophizing, right then and there, when you're least inclined and can't imagine how to do it. Performance is "how."

Picture this scene: It's at the end of a long day. Evelyn has just discovered a melted chocolate bar in the pocket of the dress that Bonny was going to wear to a birthday party tomorrow; now Evelyn will have to wash and iron it tonight. Exasperated, she's about to lose her temper. In that moment, she has a choice: She can act out the role of an angry mother (express her limited self), a part she already knows by heart, or she can give a performance of philosophizing. That is, she can question her "perfectly reasonable" (societal) assumptions

about her emotions and in doing so free herself — and Bonny
— from the limitations that they impose on what these two
human beings are able to do together.

Over the millennia professional philosophers of various persuasions have preoccupied themselves with the significance of
that transitory moment when, at the unmarked and unguarded
border where unself-conscious childhood ends and alienated
adulthood begins, we first become aware of our self-identity,
which simultaneously and paradoxically allows us to see that
we are social and distances us from our socialness. They have
sought to monumentalize that historical occasion of recogni-
tion/loss as the Moment of Truth, the beginning of the Human
Tragedy, or some other abstraction; speaking clinically, some
philosophers are madly (psychotically) obsessed with alienation
— the "split personality" that is simply a condition of normal
adult human life in our culture. Yet the vast majority of nor-
mally (neurotically) alienated/societally adapted people go
about the business of their lives without ever giving the schizophrenic existential condition of our species any thought at all.

The point is not that alienation is really a good thing, nor
that it is really bad. Alienation is no more, and no less, than the
objective product of the necessary, developmental process by
which we become adapted to society; to be a societally adapted,
properly behaved, fully self-conscious adult in our culture (and,
in varying degrees, in every culture) *is* to be alienated. What we
are alienated from is the historical, performatory social process
of creating culture — paradoxically, the very process from which
a private, individuated self-identity emerged in the first place.
Once it comes into existence the individuated self, the extraordinarily powerful societal illusion which is required to behave in
everyday life, increasingly gets in the way of the adult's capacity

to engage in historical performance.

Alienation, from this vantage point, is a condition of societal and cultural life in much the same way that gravity is a condition of physical life; regardless of how we feel about it, it's there. To insist that nothing else matters is not, in my view, an indication of extraordinary intelligence or sensitivity (as the philosophers take a sort of mad pride in believing). But to pretend that it doesn't matter at all is like trying to take flight from the top of the nearest skyscraper: you're liable to get very badly hurt.

And yet alienation itself, fundamental and normal as it is, can never be complete; it is always tempered by our knowledge of a world in which we will someday cease to exist. As we gaze self-consciously into the societal mirrors, we're unavoidably aware of the fact that there's something there — our own death — which we don't see and can't see. For seeing requires that there be a societal self to see, and with our death (the final moment of the final act of our historical performance) our self-identity dissolves. Just as our experience of our socialness is made incomplete at the moment when as children a self-identity comes into existence that impairs our capacity to perform with other people in history, so as adults our alienation is made imperfect by our awareness that what we are able to see in the societal mirrors isn't all there is.

To be or not to be? Hamlet, the quintessential tragic hero/ modern (psychological) man, is a thoroughly joyless character caught up in an endless debate with himself about which is more honorable: "to suffer the slings and arrows of outrageous Fortune," or to end his troubles by killing himself. For as Hamlet sees it, his only choices are the alienated life of a victim and a coward — someone whose self-identity is entirely determined by the fact of his mother's adulterous complicity in his father's murder, which Hamlet cannot bring himself to avenge — and non-existence. Suicide, which brings death into full view and thereby negates it, is one means of reconciling the contradiction between societal determinism and historical indeterminacy — but it is a singularly unjoyous one. To perform or not to perform! *That's* the question, if we are to have the possibility of living joyously.

Regardless of how we may try to deny death, in theory and in practice, it is not possible to do so. Nor is it necessary for living joyously. On the contrary, I believe that we can *only* experience joyousness by fully embracing the contradictory, paradoxical, ironic reality of human life: the societal fact of alienation and the historical fact of death. This is what it is to engage in the practical-critical activity that is the performance of philosophy.

When it comes to performance, very young children have an advantage over adults in that they have not yet been forced to suppress their ability to imitate. It's simply what children do, unself-consciously, in the zpd where learning leads development. In fact, it's all they *can* do; babies have few skills, habits, inclinations, or experiences of their own from which to draw, so they imitate what other people do. It's that social activity which produces self-identity.

The advantage which adults bring to performance is that, in contrast to very young children, we do have many years of experience from which we can choose what to imitate. And that includes not only our own personal life experience, but our experience as participants in our culture: the movies and plays we've seen, the books we've read, the lives other people have lived. In other words, adults have a tremendously rich variety of material — including our own self-consciousness — out of which to create a continuous life performance. The more we perform, the richer the material from which we can continue to create new performances. In returning to the poetic realm of performance from which we all started out, we come not as children but as fully self-conscious adults. The unself-conscious bliss of childhood, when we engage in pure historical performance without any awareness of ourselves as performers, is no longer possible. In embracing our alienation as fully self-conscious adults, what we can experience is joyousness.

III

THE HEALTHY LIFE

How are you? In our culture, most people are inclined to answer this question in exclusively societal terms. Having scrutinized our selves in the societal mirrors (including the institution of Psychology, the institution of Medicine, and the institution of Language itself) and seen that something appears to be wrong, we say glumly: "Not too good."

Especially if what we see might be the "sign" of something that could be terribly painful — a dying marriage, or a life-threatening physical illness (the discovery of a lie, or a lump) — we assume it's only natural to be anxious, upset, even angry. And should it turn out that our hearts *have* been broken or that we *are* gravely ill, it's not unusual in such circumstances to become panic-stricken or deeply depressed. In our culture, to be hurt or sick (particularly, but not only, when we're in great pain) has come to mean that we have the right to be miserable — which often includes the right to make others miserable as well.

When someone who is suffering behaves in ways that are self-ish and self-centered, other people may not like it but they're expected to understand; as members of our culture they share the assumption that being in emotional or physical pain is a "reason" to have a heightened concern (to be more overidentified than usual) with one's self. To most of us, how we feel emotionally and physically is a very big part of life. Indeed, for some people it's virtually all there is. A divorce, or a diagnosis of terminal illness, may signify to them not only that "my" marriage, or "my" life, is ending; it's the end of the world.

Certainly, our individual emotional and physical well-being matters greatly from the vantage point of our societal selves. How "I" am, emotionally and physically, impacts on every aspect of "my" everyday life: what "I" need to breathe, eat, see, hear and walk; the sort of work "I" am able to do; the kinds of relationships "I" can have with other people; how "I" do sex; whether "I" can have children. Historically speaking, however — that is, from the vantage point of the ongoing life of the human species — how "I" am isn't a matter of great importance at all.

No, I am *not* advocating that we forget about our selves as a moral/ethical corrective to being preoccupied with our selves. Nor am I suggesting in any way that you and I and other individual people "really" don't matter. Quite the contrary. Our emotional and physical health (like our selves themselves) is simultaneously big *and* small, both tremendously significant and of no significance whatsoever. A precondition for creating/performing a healthy (joyous) life, it seems to me, is the adoption of a philosophical attitude that is the practical acknowledgment of our societal bigness *and* our historical smallness. If we insist on taking care of only one *or* the other, thereby neglecting our historical/societal unity, we're unlikely to experience the joyousness to be found in the tangled knot where history and society join.

The cultural assumption which compels people who are in pain to see themselves only as the societal illusions/identities that the institution of Psychology, the institution of Medicine, and the institution of Language show them to be (a dependent personality, a cancer victim) deprives human beings of our historicalness and thereby dehumanizes us. It is this profoundly alienating experience which, in my opinion, greatly exacerbates emotional and physical suffering. But there's nothing at all "natural" about it.

On the contrary, I believe that the most painful moments in life provide us with an opportunity to appeal to our humanness; that is, they can be the occasion for us to challenge in practice, through the performance of philosophizing, the very assumptions that keep us tied to our roles and our places. For it is precisely in those moments when we have a heightened awareness of our selves that human beings can self-consciously choose to reorganize the totality of our lives. And in that transformed totality *everything* changes — including our experience of pain.

A PHILOSOPHY (WITH A SMALL "P") OF HEALTH (WITH A SMALL "H")

Plato has been dead for over 2,300 years, but Platonic idealism lives on in our contemporary culture. And perhaps no Ideal wields greater influence than Health — a perfect, pure abstraction against which the institution of Medicine measures our own imperfect bodies. The idea is that either you're healthy (the picture of Health), or you're not.

In fact, at any given moment of the day, the week, our lives, we're all somewhere other than at the two poles of the dualistic paradigm that has tended to dominate scientific (biology-based) medicine for the last two centuries or more: idealized Health and idealized Sickness. In other words, no one is ever perfectly well. Nor are we ever perfectly ill — that is, until the moment we die. Then, of course, we're no longer ill at all!

A physically healthy life, in my view, is not the embodiment of Health as the antithesis of Sickness. Rather, health is an activity and a process. It is a *form of life* that we create/perform continuously with all the elements that are available to us — including our culturally produced attitudes, feelings, and

174

beliefs about our bodies, our personal experience, our genetically derived strengths and vulnerabilities, the quality of the air we breathe, what and how we eat, the expertise of both traditionally trained doctors and practitioners of non-scientific medicine, our work conditions, our preferences and habits, our relationships with other people; more precisely, it is a *relational* form of life that we create, socially, with other human beings.

We all know people who behave as if they're unhappily married to their bodies, even if they rarely encounter anything more troublesome than an occasional head cold or mosquito bite. Some may express their unhappiness by smothering their "partner" with attention, demanding to know what and how it's doing every moment of the day: they're fanatic about what they eat, how much they sleep, and the quality of the air they breathe; they believe a bruise or a bellyache must mean that something terrible is going on inside of them; they're forever on the lookout for the medical specialist who will confirm their worst fears. Other people who are apparently in an unhappy marriage with their bodies act out the role of the abusive or neglectful "spouse": they adamantly refuse to exercise; they jeer at the notion that large amounts of sugar or nicotine, caffeine or alcohol, might have an impact on their well-being; they wouldn't dream of asking for help when something goes wrong, preferring to "tough it out" instead.

Most of us also know people with severe physical disabilities — the result of birth defects, illness, injury, or simply old age — who are nevertheless living joyous lives with bodies that may be uncontrollably messy, constantly in pain, overwhelmingly burdensome…bodies that may smell bad and be ugly to look at. They've learned to embrace the limitless historical possibilities open to human beings for *creating* who we are, as well as the societal limitations that impose themselves on what we can create *given* who we are.

For in life as it is lived (not in Platonic Heaven), health is likely to be very different for different people: let's say a 20-year-old college student who swims in the pool behind his parents' house every day after class; a single mother who's holding down two jobs to make ends meet; a 60-year-old man who's worked in a factory all his life.

Is it possible, then, for someone with "bad" knees, a "bad" back, or a "bad" heart to be healthy? What if you didn't have enough to eat as a child? What if you've damaged your liver or your lungs by drinking or smoking too much? In my opinion, it is. Engaging in the ongoing cultural activity of creating/performing a healthy life is not a guarantee that we'll never be sick (again). It's simply another expression of our historicalness — our uniquely human capacity to determine, collectively, who and how we are; to participate with other human beings in making meaning; to create new, relational forms of life.

I'd like you to meet Dora, who was a member of a short-term social therapy group which I led with Dr. Susan Massad at Long Island College Hospital in Brooklyn where Dr. Massad, a general internist, is now the medical director of ambulatory care. At 75, Dora is a talented artist; she's also observant, outspoken, and full of fun. Born with cerebral palsy, Dora has only limited control of most of her muscles. (She paints with her "good" hand.) These days, she's confined to a wheelchair and needs assistance to do most things (including going to the bathroom). She's unable to hold her head up; her speech is difficult to understand; she drools. Her eyesight is failing. "Don't pity me or I'll kick your ass," Dora warned the young man who had been hired to help her get around at last year's Summer Institute — an annual weekend performance exercise I lead which is sponsored by the East Side Institute for Short Term Psychotherapy. During her appearance in "The Performance of a Lifetime," the play that the participants collectively produced in the course of the weekend, Dora told us that her life is very good. "Life could be better," this truly beautiful and healthy human being acknowledged. "But I'm not complaining."

The creation/performance of our health doesn't require that we reject uncritically the discoveries and advances of scientific medicine. Such behavior is, in my view, no more creative — and no more joyous — than the uncritical acceptance of the authority of the institution of Medicine, which is the organized practice of scientific medicine. Creating/performing a healthy life does demand that we engage in the continuous practical-critical (philosophical) activity of challenging the scientific medical paradigm, including the idealization of Health, the definition of treatment as whatever fixes sick people up and gets them back to "normal," the rule governed roles of Patient and Doctor, the scientific bias of its methods. We do this not in the interests of putting a better (more "holistic") paradigm in the place of scientific medicine, but to effect a *non-paradigmatic* understanding/practice of health that is far more emergent (less rule governed) and thereby much more consistent with who we are as human beings. The ongoing production of a new way of seeing, and being, healthy — new health forms of life — is yet another way in which we continue to create (complete) our culture, including ourselves, anew.

The institution of Medicine (with a big "M")

In *Clinical Judgment*, a book written back in 1967, Dr. Alvan Feinstein argued that because "human beings differ drastically from the material studied in laboratory research...a drastically different set of investigative procedures…a new and entirely different kind of basic scientific methodology" must be created, one which isn't derived from the irrelevant methods of the laboratory. Twenty-five years later Dr. Feinstein, the Sterling Professor of Medicine and Epidemiology at Yale University School of Medicine, wrote an article in which he acknowledged that his much-admired book had had virtually no impact on the institution of Medicine.

It isn't quite accurate, in my opinion, to say that *nothing* has changed. Even if only for self-serving economic reasons, traditional medicine has been forced to reconsider its methods and its mode of organization. (The introduction of managed care is only one example.)

A greater impetus for change, however, has come from the American people themselves. Driven by their profound dissatisfaction with how they are treated, and sometimes mistreated, by institutionalized Medicine, increasingly over the last two or three decades they have been taking their health into their own hands. While preventive medicine has received little official support, tens of millions of people have nevertheless taken responsibility for their own well-being: they are exercising regularly, eating more nutritious foods, taking vitamins, and seeking out alternative treatments such as acupuncture and massage therapy. (Similarly, the tremendous popularity of self-help books in this same period has been a response — also, in my opinion, a positive one — to the dissatisfaction of ordinary people with the authoritarian and often inhumane institution of Psychology.)

The women's movement of the late '60s and early '70s was one of the engines that drove the effort to humanize scientific medicine by taking back control of women's health from the medical authorities. (*Our Bodies, Ourselves,* the widely read self-help guide to physical health written by women for women, was a product of the struggle undertaken during those years to "empower" patients.) These days, women who are diagnosed with breast cancer may be much less likely to be told that they must undergo radical mastectomies; now at least they're presented with a choice: surgery, radiation therapy, and/or chemotherapy.

Nevertheless, as Dr. Feinstein observes, the reforms in the practice of scientific medicine that have come about since the '70s haven't succeeded in *transforming* the existing disease-centric, hierarchical institution of Medicine. They failed because, in my view, they did not constitute a thoroughgoing challenge to the medical paradigm but were instead attempts to make the institution easier (at least for some people) to live with. The changes in the practice of medicine that were inspired by the women's movement, for example — many of which were opposed by the (still predominantly male) powers-that-be — simply allowed women a little room within it. The same can be said for the growing numbers of women who have become doctors over the last 25 years; they are included only on the condition that they accommodate themselves to the institution of Medicine and assimilate its patriarchal culture. Women who are unwilling to do so can only "resist" (and then only to a degree) by entering some other profession, such as nursing or chiropractic, or by choosing a career outside Medicine.

Although I believe that the reforms have some value, ultimately they work to protect the institution; in remedying particular lapses or failures, they allow the assumptions on which the culture of Medicine rests to remain more or less intact. A particularly revealing example is the inclusion in medical school training of what is called a "psycho-social" or "behavioral" component; doctors-to-be are taught that patients are to be viewed not as isolated, individual carriers of disease but as members of complex social networks (families, friendships, communities, ethnic groups) which produce relationships, habits, feelings, and attitudes — and that all of this has a profound impact on people's health. That's wonderful. What's problematic is that this perspective is a *component* of medical training (and not even a universally respected one, since there are those who consider it to be inconsistent with "hard science"); it's analogous to having developmental psychology be a branch of Psychology. For just as a human science which doesn't take development to be a fundamental characteristic of human beings is a contradiction in terms, so too, in my opinion, a theory and practice of human health which isn't rooted in the understanding that human beings are *fundamentally* social and historical is not what it claims to be.

In the latter part of the 17th century Thomas Sydenham, a prominent English physician, made what was at the time an astonishing pronouncement: *A disease is exactly the same in Socrates as it is in the simpleton*, he said.

The democratic and egalitarian implications of that quite radical statement are, in my opinion, entirely positive. Ironically, however, over the last 300 years Sydenham's liberal insight has been used as a rationale for taking the practice of health and healing away from human beings — patients *and* physicians — and for the appropriation of that life process by the increasingly research-oriented, authoritarian and technocratic institution of Medicine in thrall to an idealized scientific method. For like most other disciplines in modern times, Medicine has grown up in the religiosified and idealized belief that the "one true way" lies along the path taken by the so-called hard sciences and the professionals who practice it.

In the course of these three centuries a scientific model of medical understanding has emerged which tells physicians what it is they're supposed to look at and for; where to find it and how to see it; what to do with that evidence; how to draw implications from it — all in the name of making their practice more scientific.

Alvan Feinstein has noted that Sydenham's notion of disease — an interchangeable, fixed, nameable, individuated *thing* explainable in terms of what caused it, and treatable in itself — has come to dominate the contemporary institution of Medicine so thoroughly that to most of us (patients as well as doctors) it seems only natural to think about it in this thingified way. Yet it wasn't so very long ago that the idea of disease as something which could be abstracted from the individual human beings who were sick was virtually incomprehensible. Indeed, some clinicians of the late 17th and early 18th centuries were outraged by the suggestion. "There is no such thing as disease," a physician named Armand Trousseau objected. "There are only sick people."

There are only sick people. But Trousseau's poignant, humanistic protest got lost in the general celebration of modern Medicine's undeniable scientific triumphs; by now Sydenham's once idiosyncratic assertion has evolved into a truism. As we approach the end of this century it is routine medical practice to treat the disease as virtually everything and to relegate patients more or less to the periphery of the treatment process, systematically excluding them from participating in the activity of their own cure/health/life.

Sometimes it is even argued that, in the best of all possible worlds, patients would be entirely excluded from participating in their treatment (as they are during surgery, for example). Why should physicians have to rely on the subjective, imprecise impressions of the patient to tell them what's going on when x-rays, laboratory tests, magnetic resonance imaging, CAT-scans, and other objective sources of information about the disease are available? Or so the argument goes.

But as Dr. Feinstein has been urging for more than a quarter of a century now, "the more distinctly human...a phenomenon, the more distinctly human will be the observational system needed to identify it...the laboratory conditions of measurement do not suitably simulate the diverse challenges encountered in daily life." In other words, whatever researchers may discover in the laboratory setting is what there is to be discovered in the self-consciously constructed environment of the laboratory; the findings may be valid for that very particular "ecology," but they are not necessarily applicable, or even relevant, to the broader human environment from which it is abstracted.

Disease isolated in the laboratory is fundamentally different from the disease in (or of) a person. Human beings, who continuously construct the societal institutions that determine us and engage in the historical activity of deconstruction, are profoundly different from the experimental mice and monkeys (not to mention the inanimate laboratory petri dish or test tube) in which disease is cultivated, experimented on, measured, tested, and examined...by human beings. Consequently, the disease that is located in "Socrates" is a different process from the disease that is located in "the simpleton" — not merely different in the particulars of its societal appearance, but differently lived historically.

One trouble with the treatment of disease as a thing in itself, which is required by scientific medicine, is that it entirely lacks this historical, spiritual (human) dimension.

Rather, the institutionalized medical model employs a static, anti-historical and anti-spiritual definition of human beings as mere "points" at the intersection of two societal (naturalistic) lines, time and space. According to this definition, a person's existence is comprehensible as a thing: it has a definite, momentary beginning (birth) and a definite, momentary end (death); and it is bounded by definite physical measurements such as height and weight. That is, we are (like all other things) merely *when* we are and *where* we are. All else is scientifically irrelevant, extraneous.

What it is to be human — the unique, historical, qualitative character of our human-ness — is not included in traditional Medicine's scheme of things. "I" am identified with my body as it appears momentarily and naturalistically in the societal mirrors; who I am as a member of the human ensemble, continuously performing in history, has little or no place.

What follows from this reductionistic definition of human beings as nothing other than individuated physiological and biochemical objects is that as such we have or contain diseases somewhere inside us. The task of the doctor — who within the culture of Medicine and in the wider culture as well is identified as the active agent in the treatment of disease — is to get to it, drag it out, hold it up, explain what happened to cause it (perhaps the patient, or the patient's genes, did something wrong), and to get rid of it.

Ironically, this way of seeing (the positivist culture of Medicine) doesn't emerge from the hour to hour, day to day activity of treating people who are ill. Rather, it is imposed from on high — the laboratories where medical research is conducted by professionals who are often, in fact, less than interested in studying what their clinical colleagues actually do with patients. According to Dr. Feinstein and others, the theory and technique that medical students are taught has little to do with everyday clinical practice; they learn what's been learned about disease in the laboratories, and in the major university teaching hospitals where diseases are observed — despite the fact that much of what is relevant takes place before and after what Dr. Feinstein calls the "vignette of illness" that results in hospitalization.

Dr. Feinstein believes "the main adverse effect is that medical teaching (and learning) have become focused on the explicatory science of molecules, cells and membranes, and on use of the technologic procedures. Little or no emphasis has been given to the basic evidence (rather than the mathematical or computer models) used for clinical decisions, and on the important events and interchanges that constitute the doctor-patient relationship."

In other words, the institution of Medicine promotes a picture of the doctor-patient relationship which undermines the activity — the form of life — that human beings who happen to be doctors and other human beings who happen to be patients are engaged in together. Many practicing doctors constantly find themselves caught in a bind: the conservative, self-perpetuating, societal institution of Medicine exerts enormous pressure on them "from above" to do doctoring according to the scientific model, while "from below" patients demand to be treated much more humanely than the institution allows. This is despite the fact that patients themselves, like doctors, are captives of the medical model; they too are under the sway of the assumptions about doctoring that are dominant in our culture. Patients want the doctor to give them a diagnosis, a name for what is wrong with them, and they expect the doctor to get rid of it for them ("fix me up, Doc!"). Such assumptions obscure from both doctors *and* patients the origins of what they do together as a form of life.

Some doctors do acknowledge, usually privately, that the institution of Medicine is limited by its own assumptions and practices. From time to time a few outspoken ones like Dr. Feinstein and others even say so publicly; periodically articles and books appear, written by disenchanted doctors who are appalled by their discovery that the institution of Medicine itself often makes it difficult for them to treat patients very humanely or even very effectively. (For analogous reasons the institution of Education makes it exceedingly difficult for teachers to help children to learn, and the institution of Psychology gets in the way of clinicians attempting to help people who are in emotional pain.)

One of the most insightful and valuable contemporary critiques of the institution of Medicine that I have read is *The Nature of Suffering*, a book by Dr. Eric J. Cassell that was published in 1991. Clinical Professor of Public Health at Cornell University Medical College and an attending physician at The New York Hospital, Dr. Cassell begins his preface with the following assertion: "The test of a system of medicine should be its adequacy in the face of suffering...modern medicine fails that test...the central assumptions on which twentieth-century medicine is founded provide no basis for an understanding of suffering. Suffering must inevitably involve the person — bodies do not suffer, persons suffer...modern medicine is too devoted to its science and technology and has lost touch with the personal side of sickness."

Yet the systematically overbearing institution of Medicine makes it virtually impossible for individual physicians to change how medicine is done. Within that institution, any approach to healing which departs from those derived from scientific — quantitative, objective — research in the laboratory is strongly discouraged. (For a doctor and a patient to engage in qualitative clinical research/experimentation together, for example, is to go much too far off the beaten path.) This is in part because the financial risks are so great; the fear of malpractice suits hangs over every doctor's head. In the course of their training, medical students are constantly reminded of the legal, financial, and moral/ethical/religious constraints on experimentation; conservatism is built into the medical worldview. By the time they've got a license to practice medicine, in theory it makes sense to most doctors to do what's done — and nothing but that — in any given situation. In practice, however, it's not nearly that simple. For in practice doctors are not the scientifically detached observers of the laboratory, but human beings treating other human beings like themselves.

As medical technology has continued to advance, the institution of Medicine is becoming increasingly specialized. More and more, medicine is made to resemble the natural sciences: like astrophysics or microbiology, it is increasingly set apart from everyday life and understanding by its high-tech equipment, sophisticated methods, and esoteric language. Handed down to practitioners from the scientific heights of the research laboratory, all of this may be meaningful and coherent within the closed system of the institution. But the vast majority of patients, who are outsiders to this system and not initiated into its mysteries, are likely to find that the equipment, methods and language applied to them are painfully incomprehensible. (Having your family doctor listen to your heartbeat through a stethoscope is an entirely different experience from being placed inside a station wagon-size magnetic resonance imaging machine by a technician — someone you've never seen before and are unlikely to see again — who operates the machine from another room and may not look at you, or speak to you at all, except to issue instructions through a microphone.)

Within the culture of Medicine, this state of affairs is assumed to be highly desirable. According to the official medical worldview, the ideal patient is compliant, accepting of medical advice, non-complaining, and appreciative. The counterpart of this ideal is the highly knowledgeable doctor-as-scientist, a benign but ultimately unquestionable authority figure who holds medical records and test results "in trust" for the patient. (This fiduciary relationship is inscribed in the law, which does not allow doctors to reveal the information contained in them to anyone without the patient's permission.) Ideally, it is only at the discretion of this model doctor that such information is divulged and interpreted to the patient — who must wait to be told by the doctor (not nurses, laboratory technicians or other medical workers) that his PSA level is elevated, or that her EKG or Pap smear is abnormal, or that their child has a neurological deficit, and what it all means. Ideally, it is the doctor (and only the doctor) who knows what's wrong, what is to be done about it, and what the patient's "chances" are.

Sick people who rebel against the institution and its assumptions by seeking to play a more active role in the process — asking a lot of questions, expressing their own opinions — are officially defined as "difficult" or "bad" patients, while doctors who are at all inclined to sympathize with or support such insubordination frequently come under enormous pressure and even censure from the institutional powers-that-be. Despite this (and to their credit), in practice many ordinary doctors reject the cultural myth of the heroic scientist who slays the dragon of disease to rescue the patient in distress. In the actual treatment of patients, they tend to depart rather dramatically from the theory produced by scientific research that has virtually no connection to the experience of people who are in pain. For regardless of how alienating the societal institutions (Medicine or any other) may be, human beings are never entirely determined by them; we are continually finding ways to subvert their authority.

At the same time, our human (historical) bent for rebellion is constantly tempered by our human (societal) inclination to adapt. The institution of Medicine, buttressed by the centuries-old assumptions of Science that continue to dominate our culture as a whole, exerts enormous influence over us. In different ways and to different degrees, both doctors and patients are compelled to acquiesce uncritically in those assumptions and in the medical worldview that derives its legitimacy from them.

Central to the medical worldview is an attitude that I call *worst case scenario-ism*. This is the perspective that the worst possible thing which *could* happen in a given set of circumstances — a person with glaucoma might go blind, a person with diabetes might have to have his leg amputated, a person with breast cancer might die — should be the principal factor in determining treatment. The bottom line is: *Don't take risks!* This rule forces doctors to take the most conservative approach in such circumstances so that, if worst does come to worst, they're absolved of all responsibility. The manufacturer of the drugs involved and the hospital administration are also protected, as are the insurance companies; no one is to blame.

Within the culture of Medicine, therefore, it makes sense (to everyone concerned) that afterward the doctor must be able to say: "We did everything we could." This way they all look good in the societal mirrors.

Worst case scenario-ism is based partly on self-interest (and self-image), but it isn't entirely rational or even very self-conscious; it's how doctors, and patients, are trained to see the treatment process, including their own roles in it. This mode of understanding has everything to do with the abstraction of disease as a thing-in-itself, whose requirements come to take precedence over every other consideration.

Some patients react cynically to worst case scenario-ism, or what they perceive as their doctor's "scare tactics." Paul, a 52-year-old man who's been told by the cardiologist that if he doesn't go on a diet and stop smoking he'll be dead before he's 60, refuses to believe a word of it. "She just likes to show off," Paul says dismissively. "She wants me to think she has the power of life and death over me. But I'm no statistic. My father ate like a horse, drank like a fish and smoked like a chimney. And he lived to be 90."

While such patients indiscriminately reject the doctor's expertise along with the dire warnings, others react by resolving to obey doctor's orders religiously on the assumption that if they do they will be "saved." In fact, there are no such guarantees; the doctor is no more able than the patient or anyone else to know everything. The patient may do whatever he or she is told and the worst can still happen. Paradoxically, in refusing to participate actively in the developmental process of their own health, such patients make themselves very vulnerable; they throw out what they know about taking care of themselves.

The fact is that most of us take care of ourselves all the time, and for a good part of the time we do so competently. As in every other area of life, of course, some people are likely to be more or less competent than others. And as in every other area of life, some people are likely to have more and better resources available to them than others do: genetic factors, money, work conditions, the environment, the people with whom we live our lives, all have an impact on our physical well-being. Given all of that, we do what we can do with it — and most of us manage adequately enough. We eat, we sleep, we keep ourselves warm and cool ourselves off. Flus and hangovers, sunburn and indigestion, cuts and bruises, aches and pains... They come, and they go, taken care of by the people who have them (and the passage of time).

Doctors are formally trained not to look at it this way. After all, they typically see us only when something is wrong! We come into the doctor's office or the hospital emergency room as patients who, by cultural definition, don't know what to do — why else would we be there? And the person who is sick is likely to share this perspective. Within the culture of Medicine, this is the doctor's cue to think or say: "Look at what you've done to yourself! You don't know anything about your health. Move aside and leave this to the experts." In that moment the human being who until now has been handling things more or less well (suddenly objectified as the patient) is dismissed, denied, negated. And in that same moment the human being who has sworn "to first do no harm" (suddenly objectified as the doctor) is also dismissed, denied, negated. They are both dehumanized.

In refusing to recognize the competence of the person who is sick, moreover, the institution of Medicine undermines the treatment process itself. For the patient may in fact need nothing more to get better than the support that the doctor, as an expert, is able to give. This is not to turn the medical model on its head by insisting that the patient, not the doctor, knows best. The point is that these two human beings, the patient and the doctor, each bring something of value to the situation in which they are participants. The doctor brings his or her expertise. The patient brings his or her history.

When I say "history" in this context, I'm referring to the life history of the human being who is appearing in the societal role of patient at a given moment. This history isn't reducible to the history of the disease, the pain, the problem — or even of the patient (as recorded in multiple-choice responses to questions on a form, under the heading "medical history"). The history of the person who comes to the doctor for help is critical for comprehending what is going on. No one knows that history in the same way that the person who has lived it does — certainly not the doctor who may be examining the heart, the eye, the knee, or some other part of the patient's body for the first time, or who only sees it when it isn't working. This isn't to say that what and how people who are suffering know themselves is all there is to know. But any "understanding" of what's going on which doesn't include their account of their suffering is highly distorted.

Within the institution of Medicine, however, all that's supposed to count as evidence is the information yielded by tests. This empiricistic (idealistic) bias, which only takes into account what I-the-observer have actually perceived, negates historicalness in favor of the abstract, idealized, strictly societal "here and now." But how did we get here? What led up to now? Leaving history out isn't "objective," as those who do it argue; it's a form of subjectivity — subjectivity that is accorded a highly privileged status by the institution of Medicine. I'm not suggesting that testing has no value; certainly we are extremely fortunate to have it as one of the elements available to us in creating a healthy life. It's simply not all there is.

The 78-year-old husband of one of my patients has been told by his doctor, a urologist, that the prostate cancer for which he was being treated with chemotherapy has spread into his spine. Although there is no cure, the doctor is recommending that Mr. Miller begin a course of radiation therapy which is known to produce undesirable side effects. Mr. Miller has no pain, or any other symptoms; as he told his wife: "If I didn't know I was so sick, I'd feel fine." But the tests say he has a disease inside him…and so, therefore, his doctor (in obedience to the principles of worst case scenario-ism) is required to act accordingly.

In *Let's Develop!* I suggested that we need to ask "the development question" in every situation. Patients must learn to say: "What does it actually mean that I have this or that disease?" We ask this question not to be contentious, nor to disparage the doctor's skill or talent or expertise, but from the vantage point of continuous development. Chemotherapy? Surgery? Radiation? More tests? It depends. Is the purpose of the prescribed treatment to ensure that everyone involved will like what they see in the societal mirrors? Or is the treatment part of the historical process of creating/performing a healthy life?

The ongoing creation/performance of our health requires that we mount a philosophical challenge to paradigmism itself. Yes, I am talking — again — about the cultural activity which is the performance of philosophizing. And as you've come to see by now, to do it we need to build a Vygotskian zpd where we can engage in the kind of learning very young children do when they perform speaking: learning that leads development.

Creating/performing our health

In contrast to Medicine's anti-developmental modality of

fixing, the creation/performance of our health is a modality of development. In place of the profoundly instrumentalist, tool-for-result, identity-based behavior of treating a human being who happens to be sick as the "host" of a disease that the medical expert roots out so the patient can get "back to normal," the creation/performance of our health is a tool-and-result activity that we do with one another in a zone of proximal development. *It's the performatory, social activity of building the zpd with other human beings* which produces health, intimacy, learning — a new, relational form of life that's both developmental and joyous.

This is the story (which has no ending) of five people who participated in the joint activity of building a zpd and in doing so went (are going) beyond themselves in unexpected ways: Diane, an independent-minded and physically active woman who for a time was very seriously ill; her husband Glenn; their 17-year-old daughter Kathy; their next-door neighbor Emily, a massage therapist; and Robert, a doctor as well as one of their closest friends. Diane and Glenn have been in therapy with me for several years. When Diane got sick, they asked for my help.

Diane's history includes the fact that at 47 she's had "bad feet" for most of her life. Her feet were sore much of the time; she'd always felt more comfortable with her shoes off. Along with the aching, the soles of her feet were often numb. The lack of sensation had advantages in some situations (like walking barefoot on a hot beach), but it also had its dangers. So when she cut her foot on a piece of broken glass in the kitchen one morning, Diane didn't really feel it. She washed her foot, swabbed the cut with iodine, covered it with a large band-aid — and dashed off to the elementary school where she teaches kindergarten. That night she mentioned it to Glenn and

Kathy, but assured them that she was fine. For several days no one, least of all Diane, gave what she called her "little accident" a second thought.

But later that week, while Kathy was giving Diane a foot massage (as she often does in the evenings), she saw that the cut was much deeper than any of them had realized. Glenn and Kathy wanted to take Diane to the emergency room of a nearby hospital, but she refused to go. Showing her foot to the doctors at the hospital, or even to Robert (as Kathy had suggested), would "turn it into" an emergency, Diane told them. She preferred to take care of her feet on her own, as she always had.

However, she agreed to let Glenn and Kathy help her. For the next few weeks they washed the cut every night, put clean bandages on it, and made sure that Diane stayed off her feet as much as possible. But after two months the large red sore still hadn't healed. It was around this time that Diane came down with a bad case of the flu that was going around that winter. With the flu, the sore got bigger and started draining pus. By then Diane's foot was hurting all the time; now it swelled up and became inflamed.

This was when Glenn called Robert and asked him to come over; Robert stopped by the morning he got the phone call, before his office hours. Diane — who by this time was running a high temperature, shaking with chills, and in a great deal of pain — didn't say very much, except to keep asking for glasses of water to drink. Glenn and Kathy described what had been going on for the past three months. This led to the story (with which Robert was somewhat familiar) of Diane's lifelong difficulties with her feet. Then Robert examined her.

After a few minutes he announced that Diane needed to go into the hospital *immediately*. He wanted to culture (take a specimen of) both her blood and the pus coming from the sore on her foot to see what kind of bacteria they were dealing with and which antibiotics were likely to be most effective. Robert also suspected that Diane might have diabetes; he wanted blood drawn so he could check her blood sugar level. To Robert, Diane's unusual thirst was just one clue. Diabetes — the inability of the cells to use the glucose (sugar) that's in the blood, which results in their slow starvation — might account for several things, including the aches and pains as well as the numbness in Diane's feet, and the failure of the infection to heal. A few days later his suspicions were confirmed.

Feverish and hurting, Diane found the energy to ask Robert why he thought it was necessary for her to go to the hospital. Couldn't he take the cultures there, in the bedroom? Robert hesitated. He could. (He even had what he needed to do it with him, in his medical bag.) But then what?

In the end, Robert agreed that Diane might as well wait for the results at home. He took the cultures, showed Glenn and Kathy how to drain the sore (which had to be done several times a day), and told them he would be back the next evening. "Diane, I'm saying this to you as a doctor as well as your friend," he warned her on his way out. "This is serious. You belong in a hospital."

Diane was upset, hurt and angry. It seemed to her, she told Glenn and Kathy, that Robert was talking much more as "a doctor" than as a friend. And although he was speaking about what was best for her, she thought that what he was doing was protecting himself. She felt abandoned — as if he were more concerned with how he would feel and what he would say to other doctors should the infection get worse than he was with helping her. And if that was his main concern, she said, then she didn't want him around.

That night Glenn talked about what was going on in his

social therapy group. He told us he thought the situation might be getting out of control and he didn't know what to do. He wanted Robert to take over but he didn't want to talk Diane into anything; he was lonely and afraid, but he kept these feelings to himself so as not to worry Kathy — he was sure Diane was feeling the same way...

I suggested that a committee be formed to take collective responsibility for Diane's health. Then it would be unnecessary for Glenn (or anyone else) to know what to do, or for Robert (or anyone else) to take over. And Diane could have the support she needed without feeling that, if she allowed other people in, they would try to bully her into doing something "for her own good" that she didn't want to do. I offered to help them in whatever ways I could.

Glenn liked the idea, and when he told Diane and Kathy about it they did too. As it turned out, so did Robert — for he had felt that in speaking "as a doctor" he had not been able to be very giving to Diane. This was not an unusual experience for him, although the fact that Diane and he were friends made him more than usually aware of the limitations imposed by the role of doctor on his ability to do doctoring. Although the institution of Medicine is impervious to such contradictions, the human beings who experience them are not!

After leaving Diane, Robert had dropped the cultures off at the lab and then spent the day trying to figure out what to do next. When he talked it over with some of his colleagues, the consensus seemed to be that he was taking a huge risk. "What?" asked one doctor incredulously. "Her husband and her kid are taking care of her? Suppose the infection travels? She'll sue you for everything you're worth! Put her in the hospital — or tell her you want out."

Robert had a moment of panic. He wasn't worried that

Glenn and Diane might sue him. He was afraid that Diane would die if she didn't get the proper treatment. How could he play games with her life?

Then he began to think. Not about the infection, the flu, or the diabetes, but about Diane herself; they'd been friends since their college days and he cared for her deeply. She wasn't "irresponsible" or "obstinate" — words that some of his colleagues used in referring to "difficult" patients. She was Diane, a *person*, who at the moment was very sick. And she was right to feel that hospitals are sometimes terrible places to be... especially, Robert had to admit, for sick people. How could he help her?

When Glenn called him to ask if he would be on Diane's health committee, Robert — conflicted, skeptical, relieved — said yes. Diane, Glenn, Kathy, their friend and neighbor Emily, Robert and I had our first meeting that week.

Among the first decisions they made was that they would care for Diane at home. To some people (several of Robert's colleagues, various friends, and relatives), this appeared to be a decidedly risky and weird thing to do. It was risky, and may have been weird, but in fact what they did over the next several months in caring for Diane wasn't terribly radical; mostly it was just very hard and somewhat tedious work. Diane learned to give herself the daily injections of insulin required to help her metabolize the glucose that would nourish the cells of her body; several times a day Glenn or Kathy drained the sore of pus, cleaned and bandaged it; Robert came by two or three times a week to look at the infection and to check Diane's blood sugar; Emily set up a daily schedule of visits from friends and neighbors who came by in case Diane needed anything, so she didn't have to get up. (The plan was for her to spend the first six weeks or so in bed, or in a chair, with her foot raised). Emily herself came over every night to give Diane a back rub.

What *was* radical was the environment they created, which made it possible for these five very different people to do something together that they didn't know how to do. It was creating this zone of proximal development that turned out to be transformative in ways that no one could have predicted beforehand.

One condition for building the zpd is that it not be dominated by the societal assumptions on which people in our culture base their judgments of themselves and each other. In place of judgmentalism, what prevails in the zpd is *radical acceptance*. The members of the social ensemble do what they don't know how to do, and they accept whatever they do; they use it to continue building the environment where they can perform beyond themselves.

This isn't to say that Diane, Glenn, Kathy, Emily, and Robert didn't have assumptions or that they didn't make judgments. Robert, for example, assumed that as a doctor he did, and should, know better than anyone else what Diane needed to get well. Diane, Kathy, and Emily all had judgments about his attitude. Glenn was critical of himself, and of Kathy, for not having been more attentive to Diane — who in Glenn's judgment did not take enough care of herself.

These and all sorts of other assumption-embedded judgments were among the materials that they used to build the radically accepting tool-and-result environment of the zpd — an extraordinarily ordinary, uniquely human historical activity which is very different from the judgmental behavior that characterizes societal institutions.

Together they and I produced a performatory philosophical activity/environment — a new, relational form of life — in which Diane, Glenn, Kathy, Emily, and Robert could challenge, in practice, not only the assumptions about health and sickness, patients and doctors, treatment and cure that constitute the unspoken laws of the culture/institution of Medicine, but the myriad other cultural assumptions that pervade all of our societal institutions and as such overdetermine our behavior every minute and hour of the day: assumptions about men and women, husbands and wives, parents and children; assumptions about what it is/means to be caring, strong, responsible, sensible; assumptions about friendship, privacy, dignity, ugliness, and pain.

Among the most fundamental assumptions of Western (science-dominated) culture is that there is, and ought to be, a point to everything. As Robert said at our first meeting: "Whatever our differences, I think we all agree that the point is for Diane to get better." Everyone did agree with this entirely natural (that is, thoroughly societal) assumption. No doubt you share this assumption yourself. Of course there had to be a point to this activity! (What else would we all be doing there?) And of course (since Diane was so sick) *the* point had to be for her to get better — getting rid of the flu, healing the infection in her foot "once and for all," and bringing the diabetes under control.

I took what Robert said as the first move in a language game. *Why* was that the point? Why should *anything* be the point? *Why must everything have a point?* Isn't pointedness an alternative to development? If what you are doing is for a (to the) point, doesn't that limit what it is possible to do? If the point of education is for students to pass exams, doesn't that limit what and how they learn? If the point of sex is having an orgasm, doesn't that limit how people make love (and what they make of it)? And if the point of medical treatment is to get rid of the flu, heal the infection, control the diabetes, doesn't that limit what it is to be healthy?

What is the alternative to such tool-for-result, identity-based ("I" the Student or "I" the Teacher, "I" the Good Lover, "I" the Patient or "I" the Doctor) behavior? What about simply creating other, relational ("we") forms of life? What about engaging in activity? This is not the same as a form of life *for* "its own sake," or activity *for* "activity's sake" (those are merely other words for points), but a tool-*and*-result, continuous, ensemble *performance*: learning leading development, love-making, creating health...

Certainly, the activity of performing/creating a healthy life includes the alleviation of suffering by treating and curing disease. But I don't believe that the only point of treating people who are sick is to root out some thing called a disease which has somehow gotten inside them so that life can "get back to normal," to be just like, or as much as possible like, it was before. Surely, we want to help people to do more than that (particularly in the case of such postmodern illnesses as AIDS and cancer, for which there currently are no cures). And I don't mean this in a quantitative, or even in a quality-of-life, sense. I think we want to help people to go beyond themselves — to *live* "a head taller" than they are — physically, emotionally, and spiritually.

In challenging (deconstructing) the societal assumptions, we simultaneously create (reconstruct) our culture anew. That is, in creating new forms of life together we continue to produce (complete) the culture that produces us, and in doing so to produce (complete) ourselves. This is the developmental, creative activity in which these five perfectly ordinary (historically free and societally overdetermined) human beings participated.

What changed was the *totality* of what there was, including Diane's health — which is, of course, a part of the totality, although it isn't everything. Contrary to the most fundamental assumption of the institution of Medicine, it is the creative, performatory, historical activity of transforming the totality — and not the societally overdetermined treatment of the particular (abstracted from the totality) disease — that's curative.

Over the course of about ten weeks Diane *did* recover completely from the flu, the infection in her foot *did* begin to heal, and the diabetes *was* brought under control. She's physically healthier and stronger than she's ever been before. Not surprisingly, given their differences, Glenn, Kathy, Emily, and Robert were each transformed (they grew) in different ways. Glenn, who throughout their marriage had been in the habit of leaving everything up to Diane, became actively involved in making the decisions that affect their lives. Kathy became far more giving to her parents than the role of a teenager had ever allowed her to be. Emily, who for years has regarded doctors with disdain because "they're all so arrogant and ignorant," became capable of teaching what she knows about non-scientific medicine to Robert, a doctor who wanted to learn from her. And Robert, who as the paradigmatic good doctor had been skilled (only) in getting his patients back to normal, became confident in his ability to support people to go beyond themselves, as Diane did, to create their own treatment, their own cure, their own health.

Yet none of this was the purpose — the point — of the zpd. *They did not build it in order to help Diane's foot get back to normal.* (As far as her feet were concerned, "normal" hadn't ever been all that marvelous, anyway.) The infection in Diane's foot was simply another element — like their judgments and assumptions, the techniques of modern medicine, and whatever else, "good" and "bad," was available to them — that they were able to use for development; they didn't use development to fix up her foot. Diane's feet changed, along with everything else. Will she ever have "good" feet? I don't think anyone can know, nor is that the point. They did not create the environment to strengthen Glenn and Diane's marriage, to make Kathy a better daughter, to improve Emily's self-esteem or her professional relationships, or to make Robert a more sensitive doctor. *None of these things was the point.* Development has no point — or end.

Vygotsky observed that if you watch very young children as they engage in the joint activity of learning language, you see that they're not individuated, computer-like "brains" acquiring and storing information, but participants with adults and other children in a complex process which may get expressed in all sorts of ways by individual children but is nevertheless completely social. (This is quite contrary to what traditional Psychology has to say on the subject.)

To require, as the institution of Education does, that children learn on their own actually slows down the learning process and often makes further learning impossible. I believe that the institution of Medicine, by organizing the doctor-patient relationship in the way that it does, similarly slows down the health process and often keeps people who are sick from getting better.

The zpd, as Vygotsky first described it, is the gap between what an individual child can do on his or her own and the qualitatively more advanced things children are able to accomplish with others who are more experienced in those activities. Learning to create/perform a healthy life in a zpd requires the inclusion of doctors — just as the presence of adults is required in the joint activity of language-learning. And in a way that's analogous to the acceptance of children as members of the language community, in a health zpd, patients — who are likely to be less experienced, less expert, than doctors — are nevertheless accepted as members of the "health community" who participate in the joint activity of creating their health. In the zpd that Diane, Glenn, Kathy, Emily, and Robert built together, Robert availed himself of whatever knowledge, tools, and techniques were available; he simply refused (ultimately) to be constrained by the science-biased medical paradigm that unfortunately burdens the extraordinary achievements of modern medicine — a paradigm which has more and more to do with perpetuating the institution of Medicine, and less and less to do with the continuation of the developmental process of human health.

In other words, the institution of Medicine as it's currently organized has reached certain limits as a means of helping people. If human health is to continue to develop, therefore, it needs to be fundamentally reorganized. Am I talking about radical change? Yes. What's required, in my opinion, is nothing less than the deconstruction of the institution of Medicine and the reconstruction of a process of human health which builds with whatever may be valuable in that institution and discards all that is not. I'm not advocating that we fix up the institution as it currently exists (making Medicine more healthy) by "including" patients in a tokenistic or symbolic way, or making the sort of quantitative changes that will improve appearances. I don't think that will take us where we need to go.

This is not to suggest that modern science and the technology which has accompanied it haven't accomplished extraordinary things. Certainly the technological advances connected with the evolution of science since the 18th century have been among human beings' greatest achievements. They've obviously been of immeasurable value in medicine. Discoveries in microbiology, micropathology, biophysics and epidemiology, along with the invention of surgical tools and techniques, have saved hundreds of millions of lives and prevented the terrible suffering that until modern times was always and everywhere a fact of everyday life: childbirth, toothache, infectious disease, accidents, war injuries…I don't believe anyone can seriously question that.

What I *am* suggesting is that the way medicine has come to be understood and practiced prevents doctors from seeing patients in their historical totality; the medical paradigm thereby does not allow people who are sick to be helped as much as they could be. Moreover, the institution of Medicine is problematic not only from the patient's point of view but from the doctor's point of view. The systematic exclusion of patients from the process of their health does not only hurt *them*; it also denies doctors much needed practical and moral support.

Frequently doctors are under such enormous pressure that their inclination is to say: "I don't have time to go into that." I think they're probably right. Which is why I believe that changing the doctor-patient relationship would have a profound impact on the curative process. For it turns out to be much more efficient, as well as more curative, when the patient actively participates in creating the medicine, the treatment, the cure.

While doctors and patients may sometimes appear to be natural (that is, societal) adversaries, in history we are allies. For it is only together, in my view, that we can effectively challenge the very powerful institution of Medicine, which often stands in the way of helping people to be healthy.

Having said this, I don't think we can expect the members of the medical establishment — those who run the medical schools, the research institutes, the health and hospital corporations, and the American Medical Association — to take the initiative in overthrowing the institution of Medicine! After all, the establishment benefits from how that institution is currently organized. It's the vast majority of people who are decidedly *not* the beneficiaries of the existing arrangements — people who are sick, whether from time to time or chronically, and require some kind of medical expertise, and ordinary, practicing doctors — from whom the demand for change must come.

That won't be easy. Deeply embedded in the culture of Medicine is the assumption that when people are sick they're supposed to suspend their historicalness; there is overwhelming societal pressure — which is experienced by patients, their families, *and* their doctors — for the sick person to be removed from the stage of history, to stop living his or her life. In the societal mirror which is the institution of Medicine, the patient appears to be nothing other than the disease. Similarly embedded in the culture of Medicine is the assumption that the doctor-as-scientist must remain at an objective distance from the patient-as-disease.

I am recommending that we need to create a whole new way of organizing and understanding the process of human health. For as Dr. Feinstein, Dr. Cassell, and many, many other good doctors understand clearly, what it is to treat and know diseases is fundamentally different from what it is to treat and know human beings.

Can people learn to get better at this activity we call life? Assuredly. Can they learn to make better choices about when and what they eat, how they sleep and exercise and do sex, what to do when they do get sick or hurt? Certainly. Does that still leave open the possibility that they'll make mistakes? Yes. This is the risk we take when we make the decision to be active participants in the developmental process of living. Making that decision, and taking responsibility for the consequences — whatever they may be — is an exercise in being human. I'm convinced that it's good for our health.

THE RE-FORMING OF
EMOTIONAL LIFE

About Sigmund Freud

Not long ago I was somewhat shocked to be the subject of a front-page story in *The Stanford Weekly* for which I had been interviewed by the reporter. It was a very nice article, under the blaring headline "Stanford alum Newman reinvents psychology." Of course that's not quite accurate. I'm not looking to reinvent psychology; I think it was a mistake to invent it in the first place!

In my view, Psychology went wrong in the very beginning, when it was created in the scientific image as a systematic body of knowledge which purports to give truthful descriptions of "inner" life. Sigmund Freud, after all, didn't offer his ideas to the world as a kind of poetry but as a kind of science. As such (and unlike poetry), it had to be *about* something: mind, cognition, emotionality, psychopathology. The ego, the id, the superego, penis envy, the narcissistic personality — all of these were to be understood not as poetic metaphors, "figures of speech," but as linguistic pictures or representations of human thinking and feeling. (You may recognize this assumption as bearing a strong resemblance to the assumption that language represents or corresponds to reality.)

For a brief moment during the earlier part of this century Freud, a Viennese physician who created the method of treating madness known as psychoanalysis, was widely regarded as the Einstein of the human mind. Like Einstein, who was his contemporary, Freud too seemed to be the embodiment of modern Science; his investigations presumably revealed the laws that operate our inner universe, just as Einstein discovered the deep principles that govern the movements of the physical universe.

As I've said, I don't think anyone can deny that modern science was enormously liberating in the context of a world in which human beings had until then been largely subject to nature. Nor, in my opinion, can anyone seriously challenge the argument that psychoanalysis was enormously liberating in the context of a world in which until then mad people were routinely put in chains, tortured, burned, and drowned. The Freudian inclusion of the mad person in the quintessentially modern relationship — a civil contract between recognized persons (in this case, the doctor and the patient) — was a revolutionary expression of ideas about human rights that had been evolving in Western Europe since the early part of the 18th century.

Freud derived his theory largely from his observations and treatment of individuals whose extreme mental disturbance typically manifested itself in physical symptoms. The treatment consisted of having his patients talk to him about their dreams and their earliest memories. This symbolic material, as Freud designated it, represented their real (unspeakable) desires and fears — which he assumed (and/or discovered) were centered on sex and death. The role of the analyst was to interpret the symbols, thereby revealing the analysand's underlying (subconscious) state of mind, and in doing so to rid him or her of psychopathology.

Today Freudian theory is no longer the centerpiece of the curriculum at the institutions where mental health professionals are trained; only a handful of psychologists and psychiatrists are orthodox Freudians; psychoanalysis has been subject to the most thoroughgoing critiques, even from within the ranks of Freud's closest followers. Yet the apparent downward mobility of the Freudian paradigm — the decline in its official status — belies its continuing and overwhelming influence on the whole of Western culture.

Largely discredited in many of its particulars, Freud's compelling myth — a hodgepodge of Platonic notions and Judeo-Christian beliefs, held together by the linguistic trappings of science — submerged itself and became one with literature (particularly novels), theatre, history (the academic discipline), journalism, economics, and the other so-called social sciences, where it continues to flourish after three-quarters of a century. At the same time it became institutionalized in the less radical form of Psychology (where it can be applied to people who, being merely "neurotic," don't require the intensive, extremely time-consuming, and expensive analysis reserved for "psychotics"). But regardless of whether it appears in the guise of art or assumes the form of science, the Freudian paradigm still dominates our understanding of what emotions are and what it is to be emotionally healthy.

To me this is one of the great ironies, a tragic irony, of our collective life. A theory of the human mind invented by a medical doctor intrigued with the severe pathology he encountered in a handful of individuals (who were otherwise likely to have been permanently relegated to the asylum) has come to define what it is to be normal, well-adjusted, adapted — a definition which has had an impact on the lives of billions of human beings.

In my view the trouble with the Freudian paradigm, which purports to be a model for comprehending and treating human beings, is that it is not developmental. Like stars and atoms, the human mind is viewed by Psychology as an object produced by processes that take place in a series of stages; like the galaxies and subatomic particles, the mind is knowable from a distance by an objective observer who interprets and explains what is observed. In its ontology (the what is to be known) and in its epistemology (the how of knowing), the paradigm excludes emergent historical activity in favor of overdetermined societal appearance. That is, it leaves out what is uniquely human about human beings: our capacity for continuously creating the culture that determines us, which is what makes unlimited development possible.

Unlike the natural sciences, whose stunning achievements are directly related to the coherence between ontology and epistemology — the object and the method of study — a human science rooted in the methodological assumption that there is no such thing as development is incoherent with what it is about. It is a myth. As an element which is used in the creation of art, the myth of Psychology is often fascinating and occasionally moving. Masquerading as a science, it has been profoundly harmful to many, many people.

While the scientific model has been tremendously useful in helping us to understand and control nature, it has not proven to be very effective in helping human beings to understand and transform ourselves. Nor is there any reason, in my view, to expect that it could be — or should be, despite the very powerful assumption so prevalent in contemporary culture that the more scientific something is the better it must be.

The consequences of "Truth"

Much of what is usually defined as culture in the narrow sense (music, theatre, poetry, sculpture, painting), for example, does not purport to contain true descriptions of the world, but it is not less meaningful to us because of that. And surely most of us live our everyday lives without regard for whether what we are doing conforms to the scientific criterion of aboutness. We cook meals, laugh at jokes, go dancing, pay the bills, talk to our friends, make love, walk the dog, rear our children, and do all kinds of other things without necessarily assuming that what we are doing is really about something else and therefore subject to the truth test. They can't be true to life; they *are* life. When you look out the window and say, "What a gorgeous day!" no one is likely to ask if that statement is true or false.

But what if *nothing* we say is true or false? What if it turns out, as Wittgenstein suggested, that "truth" and "falseness" are the products of a mistaken understanding of language as being about — representing, describing, picturing — reality? What if this habit we humans have of speaking to each other is more like the chirping of birds, one of an infinite number of activities we do together which have no meaning "above and beyond" themselves but are simply *forms of life?*

In modern times the "hard" sciences have been predicated on the assumption, which as far as anyone knows is correct, that the natural world is impervious to being described. In other words, you may call a star "a red dwarf" and it will go on doing precisely what it was doing before; it will not be affected in any way by the fact of having been described or diagnosed in this way. This is not the case with human beings, however, although it is an assumption of the pseudo-science of Psychology that it is. But as Vygotsky argued, a human science must take into account the self-reflexive fact that it is human beings who study other human beings. The making of a diagnosis, the speaking of the words "learning disabled," "manic depressive," "low self-esteem," "borderline IQ," or "paranoid schizophrenic," transforms the human situation — the form of life — in which that utterance was made. Having been identified in a particular way is now part of the history of someone's life. The pseudo-science of Psychology seems incapable of comprehending that fundamental fact.

In the traditional therapeutic setting, patients or clients say something about how they feel or think and the therapist offers an alternative (competing) description (an analysis, an insight, a diagnosis) which is ostensibly truer or deeper than the client's description. To the extent that patients/clients come to accept the alternative descriptions articulated by the therapist, so the story/myth goes, they might get "better."

Indeed, people in traditional therapy often do get better and better at giving correct characterizations of their lives. A growing ability to describe or classify life, however, is not necessarily the same thing as growing, developing, getting better at living. What if it turns out, in fact, that while aboutness talk may enable us to describe life easily and comprehensibly, it's *not* very helpful to people who are in emotional pain? What if Psychology's obsession with discovering the underlying truths about their lives stands in the way of their cure?

During the last 25 years my colleagues and I have been attempting to explore those questions by creating a non-psychological method/environment that doesn't attempt to get at such "truths" but helps people to reinitiate their emotional development. My concern is not to come up with a correct critique of the myth of Psychology (which is, after all, simply a way of reinventing it), but to provide — not in theory, but in practice — an alternative to it.

The work of some contemporary critical theorists who are in the anti-Psychology tradition within traditional Psychology is, in my opinion, first-rate criticism. However, I don't believe it's enough just to have a critique of traditional Psychology — however "correct" the critique may be, however "good" the intentions of the critics. For in the absence of creating a way to help people who are in emotional pain to grow, in my view, the institution of Psychology will continue to prevail. For like all myths, the myth of Psychology is very seductive. It's familiar. It makes mental and emotional life easy to talk about in a way that seems to be comprehensible.

If we are going to have a human science which is genuinely helpful to people, in my opinion what's needed is not simply to challenge the anti-developmental conclusions that follow from the Freudian paradigm; we need to challenge the assumptions — including the assumption of paradigmism itself — on which it is based. For just as the creation of our physical health requires that we engage in a deconstruction of the medical paradigm/the institution of Medicine, in creating our emotional health we need to deconstruct the Freudian paradigm/the institution of Psychology. We do this not from the far-off standpoint of "objectivity" that is ostensibly (ideally) above and beyond societal institutions and assumptions, but in the everyday, ongoing performance of philosophizing — the practical-critical, tool-and-result historical activity of deconstructing and reconstructing the culture that produces us: in this case, our own (non-paradigmatic) psychology.

Emotional-language games and forms of life

The Freudian paradigm that so pervades traditional clinical practice (regardless of the "approach," or "school") is based on the assumption that people in therapy are emotionally disabled or impaired as a consequence of flawed relationships with their parents or traumatic events that took place in early childhood, or biochemical imbalances that were there even before they were born. The point of traditional therapy is to adapt, or adjust, patients/clients to the societal rules and roles, which is how mental health is defined; the treatment is supposed to move them in the direction of one or another Freudian-derived ideal (such as the "intact ego") — *given who they are*.

Social therapy is a non-adaptive, anti-authoritarian alternative to Psychology which helps people *to be other than who they are* — not to achieve a paradigmatic (ideal) state defined as Normal, Well-Adjusted, or Intact, but to engage in an ongoing, lifelong, developmental performance of who they aren't. In my view, it is this pointless historical activity which is mentally healthy. I am not suggesting here that societal behavior drives people "crazy." Rather, it is our forced exclusion from history — the assumption of Psychology that we are *only* our alienated, societally determined selves-identities — which is profoundly disturbing to many, many people. For in rejecting the historical dimension of human life, Psychology denies us the possibility of experiencing the joy to be found in the contradictory juncture where history and society meet. It deprives us of performing.

In social therapy we are not concerned with helping people to acquire a fixed (societal) emotional Identity, but to create ever-developing (historical) emotional activity: new, relational forms of life. We do this by building a performatory philosophical environment where we can play (in the Vygotskian sense) relational emotional-language games (in the Wittgensteinian sense). It is by participating in the practical-critical activity of collectively challenging/deconstructing the identity-based assumptions of Psychology and of Language — like the assumption that emotions are things inside "me" and "you" which language is about or represents or expresses — that the members of the social therapy group create their own psychology: new emotions, new diagnoses, new forms of life.

The playing of emotional-language games, the self-conscious performance of philosophizing which is the activity of the social therapy group (although of course it is not the only thing that goes on there), is among other things an alternative to Philosophy. For while Philosophy challenges the societal assumptions with its own institutionalized set of assumptions, language games aren't necessarily rule governed. The emotional-language games that we play in the social therapy group are a self-conscious effort to imitate what happens unself-consciously and unsystematically in the zpd of early childhood. It's not the same, because the members of the group aren't children. But as self-conscious adults they simultaneously create a form of life together and the language (the linguistic activity) of it.

And since there isn't just one emotional language, but a whole array of them — the language/forms of life of anxiety, the language/forms of life of depression, the language/forms of life of panic, and many more — we play emotional-language games that are specific to each of those.

Contrary to our culturally drawn picture of emotions as things that exist inside individuals, in fact they originate as forms of life, relational activities, which human beings do together. It is only subsequently that an individuated mode of discourse, a way of talking, is superimposed on these relational forms of life, overdetermining what anxiety, depression, panic, and other emotions are (including when and how we feel them).

Oh, I get it! you may be thinking. *You're saying that emotions are just a matter of semantics.* Yes, I am saying that… although without the "just." For "just a matter of semantics" understates how thoroughly our understanding of emotionality is influenced by language. Talking about anxiety in the way that people in our culture typically do, for example, produces the experience of anxiety that people in our culture typically experience. In social therapy we have discovered that the playing of Wittgensteinian language games is curative; in deconstructing the language of anxiety, depression, panic, we simultaneously deconstruct the institutionalized (alienated) forms of life that are the subtly varied emotions of Anxiety, Depression, Panic. We deconstruct forms of alienation and reconstruct new forms of life.

The members of the social therapy group create a new, relational form of life/a philosophical performatory environment which challenges the identity-based, overly linguistic (alienated, language-ified) understanding of emotions that prevails in our culture. In social therapy, we're trying to create/perform a new "anxiety form of life," a new "depression form of life," a new "panic form of life" — a new emotionality that isn't completely overdetermined by the language of those emotions.

In "real" (that is, non-performatory societal) life, when someone says "I feel like killing myself," for example, that statement is typically taken by the person to whom it has been said — a friend, a relative, a therapist — as being somehow more fundamental, more serious, "deeper," than other things

that people say, and as such to require a response which is
somehow more fundamental, more serious, and "deeper" than
usual. That is, suicide/suicide talk is yet another form of life
(form of alienation) that people in our culture typically do
together in a particular way.

How might the social therapist use such a statement to
create a new form of life with someone who is feeling suicidal?
By treating it as a line in a performance piece that we're creating, then and there, with the person who spoke it.

PATIENT:

I want to kill myself.

SOCIAL THERAPIST:

I want to whistle "Yankee Doodle."

PATIENT:

This is not a joke!

SOCIAL THERAPIST:

It is if we make it one.

PATIENT:

Did you hear what I said a moment ago?

SOCIAL THERAPIST:

Yes.

PATIENT:

Why are you ignoring me? Don't you care?

SOCIAL THERAPIST:

Let's create our caring rather than judge it.

Clearly, this is a very different performance/form of life/
emotionality from what typically follows from the declaration
"I want to kill myself." These two human beings are creating

something new together, and can continue to do so endlessly; life can take infinite forms.

In the social therapy group, we play emotional-language games to strip away the Reality metaphysics of the language we use to speak about emotions. In playing this sort of language game, members of the group self-consciously challenge the ontological/epistemological assumptions embedded in emotional discourse. One such assumption is that the words "I" say to "you" convey (describe/correspond to/are the outer representations of) "my" private, internal emotional state, and that the words "you" say back to "me" similarly represent "your" private emotional property. Regardless of the content of emotional discourse — whether it's "I love you!"/"I love you, too!" or "I'm so ashamed of you!"/"I wish you were dead!" — the form of it is typically identity-based, referential, truth-bearing, and competitive.

In fact, however, neither "I love you!"/"I love you, too!" nor "I'm so ashamed of you!"/"I wish you were dead!" is merely an exchange of information about individual emotional states. Emotional discourse is the expression of a form of life — a relational form of life — which gives rise to it. That is, the meaning of emotional language comes out of a life experience that human beings create together, a shared, social experience which turns out to be not "mine" and "yours," or "mine" versus "yours," but *ours*; the historical (in contrast to both the ideal and the grammatical) subject of emotional discourse is neither "I" nor "you" but "we."

It is this joint "we" which is the author of a relationship that has meaning for us in much the same way that a mother and her baby, jointly participating in the zpd, together make a conversation that is meaningful to them. In other words, in creating a relational (emotional) form of life, we do not simply behave in the role determined, rule governed ways required of fully adapted/alienated adults; we're simultaneously engaging in a poetic, performatory (meaning-making) historical activity. The assumptions embedded in linguistically overdetermined emotional discourse serve to disguise this historical dimension of human life; the activity of playing emotional-language games reveals it.

In building the social therapy group, members of the group self-consciously create a shared experience, a relational form of life. At the same time, they create the emotional language which gives expression to — is inseparable from — that social activity, a new language (and a new psychology, with new emotions) to replace the competitive, identity-based, societally overdetermined language of "I"/"you" (and the competitive, identity-based, societally overdetermined psychology which such language validates and reinforces). We do this not to negate society, but as a way of bringing members of the group "back to" history; playing language games is the practice of a method for curing people of their alienation in a culture where Language is among the most alienating of societal institutions. That is, they engage in a completitive, relational, non-referential, non-causal discourse that isn't based on the assumption of self-identity which requires that "you" and "I" have the same emotional experience or that one of us be right and the other wrong; instead, "we" make a poem/a new (relational) psychology together.

Vicky, a woman now in her early thirties, is in the habit of pulling her hair out of her head (literally) during the periodic bouts of anxiety from which she has suffered since she was a teenager. Deeply ashamed of this behavior, she recently began talking about it in her social therapy group when the subject of "secrets" came up.

"I can't stop tearing my hair out," Vicky said.

"What do you mean by can't?" Bill, another member of the group, asked.

When Vicky didn't respond, Bill quickly added: "Are you saying that you're physically unable to prevent your arm from reaching up and tearing your hair out?"

"I mean that I can't," Vicky finally said in a choked-up voice, her face flushing.

Although Bill told us later that he'd intended to play a language game with Vicky, she told us she had heard what he said as a criticism or a judgment: *What do you mean, you can't stop...?* That she should make this assumption was perhaps unfortunate, but not surprising. For it is typical in our culture for conversation in general, and therapeutic discourse in particular, to take a competitive form which often looks like this: "I" make a statement, and "you" tell me whether (in your opinion) it is true or false, right or wrong. Traditional therapeutic discourse, in fact, is often "played" as a highly rule governed game in which, paradoxically, the patient must ultimately "lose" to the therapist (by conceding that the therapist's statements about the patient's life are superior representations of reality) in order to "win" (that is, to be cured).

"What else can't you do?" I ask in a non-provocative tone of voice.

In saying this, I'm not making a statement which, explicitly or implicitly, claims to have greater truth-value than the statement that Vicky made. I'm not competing with her, but completing for her; I'm using what she said as an element with which she and I and other members of the group can build something, although we don't know what that is and there is no blueprint for it. I'm asking a philosophical question, which might lead to the group's collective discovery that the only thing Vicky thinks she can't do is to stop pulling her hair out, or that this is one of many things she can't do. And that might lead to an exploration of what she thinks she can do, needs to do, wants to do, does and doesn't do. Or it might be that Vicky thinks she can't do anything, which in turn might lead to an exploration of how she sees what we're doing together in having that dialogue. Or it might not lead anywhere at all. In creating our collective poem, or play, we don't necessarily produce something wonderful every time we do it.

I don't have the "right" answer to my question, which Vicky has to get. I'm not trying to show her that in pulling her hair out she's really rejecting her femininity or punishing her parents; I'm not attempting to say something about her which is more true or more profound than what she has said; I'm not seeking to fit her symptoms into a diagnostic category; I don't know what her "problem" is; I don't know, nor am I pursuing, the solution to it. In other words, as a social therapist I'm not doing the pseudo-science of psychology by "getting to the bottom" of things. Rather, Vicky and I and the other members of the social therapy group are engaged in the "shallow" cultural activity of making something together which is not about (does not mean) anything else. It simply is what it is: a collective performance, a social activity, a new and emergent form of life.

Changing the diagnostic form of life

Social therapy is not in the business of diagnostics. The social therapist is not an authority figure who labels, categorizes, explains, interprets, or otherwise analyzes people's psychopathology, and then tells them the solution to their emotional "problems." While labeling, categorizing, explaining, interpreting, diagnosing — practices borrowed by psychology from traditional medicine, which in turn took them from the natural sciences (where they have been, no doubt, of enormous value in solving all kinds of problems) — may occasionally be of some use to people suffering from physical illness or injury, the imposition of official labels/identities on people who are in emotional pain primarily serves to prop up the myth of Psychology; in my opinion, it's rarely useful. And all too frequently it does irreparable damage.

In doing therapy it's often obvious to me, even in the very first session, what is "wrong" — I'm able to see in the narrative people give of their lives what it is that's producing their emotional pain. (Many other clinicians have this experience as well.) Yet it can sometimes take a good deal of time for me, together with the person who is in pain, to create the tool-and-result historical environment in which that pain can be touched, and treated — the environment in which that person can be cured.

In other words, it's possible to know something cognitively about someone in therapy (as in the rest of life) almost immediately, yet not be able to create anything of value with that knowledge for a very long time. So it may be necessary to do the first session over and over — and over — again.

But that's a waste of time! you rationalists may object. I don't believe it is. For it's the sheer activity of repeating (not in the sense of mimicking, but creatively imitating) that session — like performing King Lear over and over again — which is itself the developmental process. Social therapy works to the extent that it is the constant, collective activity of re-creating not only people's "pathology" but social therapy itself. We're not concerned to preserve the myth that Psychology is a systematic, explanatory science by using people's emotional "problems" as evidence to prove the validity of psychological "laws." Social therapy has no laws. Rather, we're engaged in a distinctly cultural activity which is like the collective creation of a poem; its meanings are not defined beforehand but are produced in the process of creating it.

This is the activity of building a zone of proximal emotional development where the social therapist can complete for, not compete with, the people "in" the group, who are thereby supported to go beyond themselves; as members of the social ensemble, they are "extended." They do what they don't (couldn't) know how to do emotionally, and in doing so create their own emotionality and their own psychology — including their own diagnoses. For it's not diagnosis, in my view, but the authoritarian, pseudo-medical, pseudo-scientific "truth" of it that does harm. (That medical diagnoses, by contrast, are often useful and helpful simply points to the difference between science and myth. Scientific medicine is not as helpful to people as it could be as a consequence of how the institution of Medicine is organized. Traditional Psychology, however, is merely a pseudo-science.) Social therapy isn't a negation of diagnostics but a re-creation of it; it's a transformation of the diagnostic form of life. For if *everyone* is doing diagnosing in a radically democratic, performatory environment, then diagnosis is no longer what it is — and so it's no longer problematic.

Certainly it's a very different enterprise indeed from the role determined, rule governed cognitive behavior of describing and prescribing that characterizes traditional clinical psychology. Deeply invested in the societal identity of a knower and invoking the higher authority of knowledge, the traditional psychologist can only apply the psychology that is already there to the less knowledgeable patient.

In social therapy, we all perform diagnosing together —

not to get it right, and not even to give everyone a chance at it. We do it in the joint activity of creating/performing a zone of proximal emotional development in which our varied forms of emotional life can, through collective performance, create new forms of life, new meanings, new lives. It is this joint developmental activity of building a "zped" where the social therapist and the people "in" social therapy are together creating a new psychology, new emotions (a new poetic), that we have found to be curative.

It has recently become faddishly fashionable, in some liberal academic circles, to poke fun at the American Psychiatric Association's *DSM-IV*, a colossal 900-plus pages filled with categories and sub-categories and sub-sub-categories (all of them duly numbered) describing the zillion and one ways in which people can be mad or sad. However the problem with diagnoses, it seems to me, is not that they're silly or inaccurate — "bad" or "false" — pictures of human emotionality (although, to be honest, I think most of them are), but with the method which produces them.

For if language is a social activity that people do together and not something which paints a picture of something else, then it's not possible for anyone — the scientist, the therapist, the man, the adult — to have the right answer, the correct diagnosis, the superior analysis; there simply isn't such a thing! So I'm less interested in criticizing the *DSM-IV* than I am in challenging the authoritarian, patriarchal, dualistic, idealistic "science" that requires it. I don't want to get rid of diagnoses, or to come up with better ones, but to change what diagnosing is.

Actually, it seems to me that we might need more diagnoses, not fewer ones. But I think everyone should be allowed to do diagnosing, all the time. We need to be constantly re-characterizing, re-describing, re-seeing our lives — not from the vantage point of coming up with the Truth, or even with "truths," in the pseudo-scientific manner of Psychology, but as a performatory activity…a form of life in which everyone, not just the officially designated experts, have the authority to do it.

Performance vs. Truth

What we create in social therapy is a democratic relational process/environment which is not dominated by a figure who is in a special position, by virtue of being an authority, to know the truth about life. It is a performatory activity/environment to which some people may give their special therapeutic expertise just as others give what *they* have to give.

In such a performatory environment, truthfulness is not a relevant criterion. The members of the social therapy group are not doing something that is "really" about something else, just as performers in a play aren't doing something that is "really" about something else; they're performing. When an actor in a play says: "The night is dark, and silent…," the other actors and members of the audience don't interrupt to say: "Look outside! It's broad daylight, the sun is shining, birds are singing." When Carmen says she loves the toreador, the boyfriend of the opera singer who's performing the part of Carmen doesn't typically storm out of the theatre in a huff.

Similarly, in relating to what people do when they speak to each other as a performance, the social therapist is attempting neither to utter truths about life nor to judge the truth value of what other people say, but to create a social interaction with them which *is* life (a new form of life). That is, performance creates — is a showing of — language as activity. Unlike the traditional therapeutic environment, performance does not require a standardized diagnostic and statistical manual of mental disorders.

Social therapy helps to revitalize the performatory dimension of life. Every week, the members of the social ensemble that is the therapy group create a play together — perhaps several plays. This is not a metaphor; they are not "really" and "truly" doing psychology (disguised as theatre). It is not performance (Gestalt or primal or otherwise) *in* therapy but *therapy as performance*.

What do people get out of performing? What's the therapeutic point of it all? In performing people come to see that they *can* perform. They learn, together with the other members of the group, that they can collectively create something new with what they're given (including their pathology and their pain); they can make up endless and endlessly imaginative performances of their lives. *They can produce culture.* That recognition of our human capacity to transform situations is enormously valuable.

For often what makes an emotionally painful experience so painful is the assumption (whether it's stated or not) that there's no way to get out of the situation, and in particular no quick way to get out of it. In performance you see that it's possible to create something new "on the spot." You can *perform your way out* of all sorts of emotional situations you don't want to be in: going through a divorce; having to work under someone who doesn't know her business as well as you do; finding out that your unmarried 17-year-old daughter is pregnant; grieving over the death of someone you loved; quarreling with a friend; feeling lonely at a party; worrying about money; becoming seriously ill…

Performance can be very hard work. But anyone can do it, anywhere and at any time. A stage, after all, is only the floor and the lights raised a bit so that the actors can be seen by the rest of us.

I'm not suggesting that we can do (or undo) whatever we want to. The point I'm making is that from a performatory point of view, an infinite variety of possibilities is open to us in every situation. Performance challenges the myth that people are only who they already are, mentally and emotionally, as defined (diagnosed) by Psychology.

Back to history

My work as a social therapist has been successful largely, I believe, as a direct consequence of the fact that the people who are "in" social therapy actively participate in the ongoing cultural activity of continuously creating a new psychology that can be helpful to them. I don't make the assumption that some people are too incompetent, too crazy, too disturbed, too angry (or too anything else) to participate with me in the joint activity of creating their cure. Everyone is included; anyone can play.

Language games are a means for "reintroducing" self-conscious, societally overdetermined adults to their historicalness. Playing them enables members of the social therapy group to see the origins of language as activity, a form of life in which they participated unself-consciously as very young children. Paradoxically, it is our participation in this unruly poetic activity of making meaning in the tool-and-result, social environment of the zpd that enables us to become adapted to the tool-for-result, societal institution of Language — that is, to engage in the prosaic, role determined and rule governed behavior of using the meanings that are already there. Yet in becoming fully adapted to society we are in that moment alienated from history. As self-conscious adults we reject performance in favor of behavior; we're unable to see ourselves as the historical makers of meaning.

It's not a matter of good or bad, as I said earlier. In social therapy we are not trying to prove that there's something "wrong" with society/behavior. (Social therapy is not in the coercive business of proving, or explaining, or interpreting, anything.) Rather, the playing of emotional-language games is a *showing* of historical performance. In particular, such language games allow members of the social therapy group to *see* themselves creating/performing "a head taller" (as Vygotsky put it) then they are emotionally.

What is the value of such showing/seeing? It is by performing ahead of ourselves, remember, that we human beings develop. As you saw close-up in the chapters on learning and performing, the very young child performs in history but — lacking self-consciousness — cannot experience the joy, or the alienation, of seeing "my self" perform. The self-consciously alienated adult, by contrast, constantly sees "my self" in the societal mirrors but — in the absence of performing — can only experience alienation, not the joy of seeing "my self"/being in history. The playing of emotional-language games, in recalling self-conscious adults to their historicalness, allows them to go beyond development; it opens the door to living joyously.

No, it is not the "examined" life which is worth living (as self-congratulatory professional thinkers like to believe). It is the performatory life — with its possibility of living joyously — which *is* living.

What childhood is to children, philosophizing is to adults

As "normal" — fully adapted/alienated — adults in our culture, most of us are painfully estranged from ourselves; "I" can only know myself as I appear in the societal mirrors. (It's like gazing at an old family photograph, trying to glimpse in the facial expressions or posture of people who died long ago something about their lives.) By contrast, living joyously requires that "I" be fully intimate with the human being who is me: the individuated, societally overdetermined product of our culture, *and* a member of the social ensemble which collectively creates culture. To live joyously, in my view, is to relinquish the deadening stability of alienation in favor of the thrilling, gut-wrenching, giddy, and terrifying experience of continuously being and seeing who we are in all its complex, conflicted contradictoriness. Yes, we are completely shaped by our culture's assumptions — and we are completely free to challenge them.

Very young children are constantly challenging the cultural assumptions through their activity, which is not yet constrained by the self-consciousness acquired in the process of adaptation; they are like visitors to a foreign planet where every custom, the meaning of every word, and every explanation (including the custom of having customs, the meaning of meaning, and explaining) are utterly strange. In performing philosophy adults — who are subject to the role determined, rule governed constraints imposed by Language and the other societal institutions — self-consciously challenge customs, meanings, explaining, and every other cultural assumption; they ask big questions about little things, just as the youngest children do. (Why don't ants talk? Etc., etc., etc.)

Philosophizing is the ground from which we, as adult human beings, can call into question the most obvious, goes-without-saying givens of our culture. Philosophizing thereby makes it possible for us to return to the performatory realm of history — not as unself-conscious children but as the self-conscious adults we are. It is in this sense that philosophizing is to adults what childhood is to children; it is the condition for historical, performatory activity.

Existentialists could argue that despair, not joy, is the appropriate response to the recognition that we have nothing but our freedom — Existentialism being a "school" of Philosophy which rests on the assumption that each of us is alone in a purposeless universe where a random act of brutality has no more "meaning" than a random act of kindness. *Aren't you making a virtue of necessity?* the Existentialist may ask, accusingly.

Yes, and no. In my view, joyousness is to be found in the actuality of human life — not in an idealization or a fantasy of it. I think we need to seek out the contradiction at the heart of what Existentialists call "the human condition" to see what we can create with it. This is not to valorize, or deny, Death (or any individual death); it's simply what there is to do, while we are here, given that we *are* here and given who each of us is: the living repository of the cultural conflict between history and society, neither so overdetermined by the societal assumptions that we stop performing, nor so lacking in self-consciousness as to assume that we're gods.

The actor who gives a great performance of King Lear does so not by virtue of coming to believe that he really is Shakespeare's tragic figure. The greatness of the performance lies in the actor's full awareness that he, the actor, is giving/creating a performance of King Lear. Performance is not the negation of our selves; it's the self-conscious giving/growing of who we are. That's the joy of it.

The developmental process of going beyond yourself is not the same as going to Something — Heaven, or immortality; it's the continuous, ongoing doing of the impossible. What's joyous is to engage in that historical performance while recognizing the societal impossibility of it — and continuing to give it all we've got: undaunted, absurd, flamboyant, always smilingly aware of our smallness.

No, smallness is not beautiful. Nor is bigness. But there is, in my opinion, an exquisite joy in the uniquely human predicament of being both big and small (and everything in between); of knowing so much and yet so little; of controlling a good deal and nothing at all. We are rare birds and we must enjoy our enigmatic social selves much as birds appear to enjoy flying together. It is, ultimately, a matter of life *and* death. To paraphrase Wittgenstein, the nicest thing about death is that we don't live through it. And to quote Frank Sinatra, "That's Life."

BIBLIOGRAPHY

American Psychiatric Association. *Diagnostic and Statistical Manual of Mental Disorders*. 4th ed. Washington, D.C. American Psychiatric Association, 1994.

Aristotle. *The Basic Works of Aristotle*. Edited by R. McKeon. New York: Random House, 1941.

Austin, J.L. *How to Do Things with Words*. Oxford: Oxford University Press, 1962.

————. *Sense and Sensibilia*. Oxford: Oxford University Press, 1962.

Baker, G.P. *Wittgenstein, Frege and the Vienna Circle*. Oxford: Blackwell, 1988.

————. "Some Remarks on 'Language' and 'Grammar.'" *Grazer Philosophische Studien* 42 (1992): 107-131.

Baker, G.P. and Hacker, P.M.S. *Wittgenstein: Understanding and Meaning*. Oxford: Blackwell, 1980.

Boal, Augusto. *Theatre of the Oppressed*. Translated by Charles and Maria-Adalia Leat McBride. New York: Urizen Books, 1979.

Brecht, Bertolt. *Brecht on Theatre*. Edited and translated by John Willett. New York: Hill and Wang, 1964.

Cassell, E.J. *The Nature of Suffering and the Goals of Medicine*. New York: Oxford University Press, 1991.

Chomsky, Noam. *Syntactic Structures*. The Hague: Mouton, 1957.

Cole, M. "Cultural Psychology: Some General Principles and a Concrete Example." Paper presented at the Second International Congress of Activity Theory. Lahti, Finland, 1990.

Davidson, D., Suppes, P., Siegel, S. *Decision-Making: An Experimental Approach*. Stanford: Stanford University Press, 1957. [Reprinted by the University of Chicago Press, Chicago, 1977.]

Davidson, D. "On the Very Idea of a Conceptual Scheme." *Proceedings and Addresses of the American Philosophical Association* 67 (1973-74): 5-20.

————. "Actions, Reasons and Causes." In *Essays on Actions and Events*. Oxford: Clarendon Press, 1980.

Derrida, J. *Of Grammatology*. Baltimore: Johns Hopkins University Press, 1976.

Dray, W. *Laws and Explanation in History*. London: Oxford University Press, 1957.

Feinstein, A.R. *Clinical Judgment*. Baltimore: The Williams and Wilkins Company, 1967.

————. "An Additional Basic Science for Clinical Medicine: I. The Constraining Fundamental Paradigms." *Annals of Internal Medicine* 99 (1983): 393-397.

————. "An Additional Basic Science for Clinical Medicine: II. The Limitations of Randomized Trials." *Annals of Internal Medicine* 99 (1983): 544-550.

————. "An Additional Basic Science for Clinical Medicine: III. The Challenges of Comparison and Measurement. *Annals of Internal Medicine* 99 (1983): 705-712.

————. "An Additional Basic Science for Clinical Medicine: IV. The Development of Clinimetrics. *Annals of Internal Medicine*. 99 (1983): 843-848.

Foucault, M. *Madness and Civilization: A History of Insanity in the Age of Reason*. New York: Pantheon, 1965.

————. *The Birth of the Clinic: An Archeology of Medical Perception*. New York: Vintage Books, 1975.

Frege, G. *The Foundations of Arithmetic*. Translated by J.L. Austin. Oxford: Blackwell, 1950.

Freud, S. *Basic Writings of Sigmund Freud*. Translated and edited by A.A. Brill. New York: Modern Library, 1938.

Gergen, K.J. *Toward Transformation in Social Knowledge*. London: Sage, 1982.

————. *The Saturated Self: Dilemmas of Identity in Contemporary Life*. New York: Basic Books, 1991.

————. *Realities and Relationships: Soundings in Social Construction*. Cambridge: Harvard University Press, 1994.

————. "Social Construction and the Transformation of Identity Politics." Paper presented at the New School for Social Research, New York City, 1995.

Gleick, J. *Chaos. Making a New Science*. New York: Penguin Books, 1987.

Gödel, K. *On Formally Undecidable Propositions of Principia Mathematica and Related Systems*. London: Oliver and Boyd, 1962.

Habermas, J. *Knowlege and Human Interests*. Boston: Beacon Press, 1971.

Hampshire, S. *Thought and Action*. London: Chatto and Windus, 1959.

Hempel, C. *Aspects of Scientific Explanation*. New York: The Free Press, 1965.

Holzman, L. "Notes from the Laboratory: A Work-in-Progress Report from the Barbara Taylor School." *Practice, the Magazine of Psychology and Political Economy* 9 (1993): 1, 25-37.

————. "Creating Developmental Learning Environments: A Vygotskian Practice." *School Psychology International* 16 (1995): 199-212.

Kant, I. *Critique of Pure Reason*. New York: St. Martin's Press, 1965.

Kenny, A.J.P. *Action, Emotion and Will*. London: Routledge and Kegan Paul, 1963.

Kuhn, T. *The Structure of Scientific Revolutions*. Chicago: University of Chicago Press, 1962.

Lewis, C.I. *Mind and the World Order: Outline of a Theory of Knowledge*. New York: Dover, 1990.

Lovejoy, A.O. *The Revolt Against Dualism: An Inquiry Concerning the Existence of Ideas*. 2d ed. LaSalle: The Open Court Publishing Co, 1960.

Melden, A.I. *Free Action*. London: Routledge and Kegan Paul, 1961.

Newman, F. *The Myth of Psychology*. New York: Castillo International, 1991.

————. "Philosophical Meanderings on Medical Methodology." Paper presented at Long Island College Hospital, Brooklyn, New York [manuscript available], 1993.

Newman, F. and Gergen, K.J. "Diagnosis: The Human Cost of the Rage to Order." Paper presented at the 103rd Annual Convention of the American Psychological Association, New York City [manuscript available], 1995.

Newman, F. and Holzman, L. *Lev Vygotsky: Revolutionary Scientist*. London: Routledge, 1993.

Newman, F. and Holzman, L. *Unscientific Psychology. A Cultural-Performatory Approach to Understanding Human Life*. Westport: Praeger, in press.

Parker, I. *The Crisis in Modern Social Psychology and How to End It*. London: Routledge, 1989.

————. *Discourse Dynamics*. London: Routledge, 1992.

Parker, I. and Shotter, J. *Deconstructing Social Psychology*. London: Routledge, 1990.

Peirce, C.S. *Essays in the Philosophy of Science*. New York: The Liberal Arts Press, 1957.

Peterman, J.F. *Philosophy as Therapy: An Interpretation and Defense of Wittgenstein's Later Philosophical Project*. Albany: SUNY Press, 1992.

Piscator, E. *The Political Theatre*. Translated by Hugh Rorrison. New York: Avon Books, 1979.

Plato. *The Collected Dialogues of Plato, Including the Letters*. Edited by Edith Hamilton and Huntington Cairns. Princeton: Princeton University Press, 1961.

Quine, W.V.O. "Two Dogmas of Empiricism." In *From a Logical Point of View*. 2d ed. New York: Harper & Row, 1961.

————. *Word and Object*. Cambridge: MIT Press, 1960.

Rorty, R. *Consequences of Pragmatism*. Minneapolis: University of Minneapolis, 1982.

Ryle, G. *The Concept of Mind*. New York: Barnes and Noble, 1949.

Russell, B. *The Problems of Philosophy*. London: Oxford University Press, 1912.

Sampson, E.E. "The Democratization of Psychology." *Theory and Psychology* 1 (1991): 275-298.

————. *Celebrating the Other: A Dialogic Account of Human Nature*. Boulder: Westview Press, 1993.

Schacht, T.E. "DSM-III and the Politics of Truth." *American Psychologist* 40 (1985): 513-521.

Scriven, M. "Truisms as the Grounds for Historical Explanation." In *Theories of History,* edited by P.L. Gardiner. Glencoe: The Free Press, 1959.

Searle, J. *Speech Acts: An Essay in the Philosophy of Language*. Cambridge: Cambridge University Press, 1969.

————. *The Rediscovery of Mind*. Cambridge: The MIT Press, 1992.

Shakespeare, W. *The Tragedy of Hamlet, Prince of Denmark*. In *The Complete Works of William Shakespeare*, edited by W.A. Wright. Garden City: Doubleday, Doran & Company, 1936.

Shotter, J. "A Sense of Place: Vico and the Social Production of Social Identities." *British Journal of Social Psychology* 25 (1986): 199-211.

————. *Knowing of the Third Kind*. Utrecht: ISOR, 1990.

————. "Wittgenstein and Psychology: On Our 'Hook Up' to Reality." In *Wittgenstein: Centenary Essays*, edited by A. Phillips-Griffiths. Cambridge: Cambridge University Press, 1991.

———. *Conversational Realities: Studies in Social Constructionism*. London: Sage, 1993.

———. *Cultural Politics of Everyday Life: Social Constructionism, Rhetoric and Knowing of the Third Kind*. Toronto: University of Toronto Press, 1993.

———. "In Conversation: Joint Action, Shared Intentionality and Ethics." *Theory and Psychology* 5(1)(1995): 49-73.

Shotter, J. and Gergen, K.J., editors. *Texts of Identity*. London: Sage, 1989.

Shotter, J. and Newman, F. "Understanding Practice in Practice (Rather Than in Theory)." Paper presented at the East Side Institute for Short Term Psychotherapy, New York City [manuscript available], 1995.

Strawson, P.F. *Individuals*. London: Methuen, 1959.

Szasz, T. *The Myth of Mental Illness: Foundations of a Theory of Personal Conduct*. New York: Harper & Row, 1961.

Tarski, A. *Logic, Semantics, Metamathematics; Papers from 1923 to 1938*. Translated by J.H. Woodger. Oxford: Clarendon Press, 1956.

Vickers, J.M. "Objectivity and Ideology in the Human Sciences." *Topoi* 10(2)(1991): 175-186.

Vygotsky, L.S. *Mind in Society*. Cambridge: Harvard University Press, 1978.

———. *Thought and Language*. Cambridge: MIT Press, 1986.

———. *The Collected Works of L.S. Vygotsky*. Vol. 1. New York: Plenum, 1987.

———. *The Collected Works of L.S. Vygotsky*. Vol. 2. New York: Plenum, 1993.

Waldrop, M.M. *Complexity. The Emerging Science at the Edge of Order and Chaos*. New York: Touchstone, 1992.

Wittgenstein, L. *Philosophical Investigations*. Oxford: Blackwell, 1953.

———. *Blue and Brown Books*. Oxford: Blackwell, 1958.

———. *Tractatus Logico-Philosophicus*. London: Routledge, 1961.

———. *Zettel*. Oxford: Blackwell, 1967.

———. "Remarks on Frazer's 'Golden Bough.'" *The Human World* 3 (1971): 28-41.

———. *Philosophical Grammar*. Oxford: Blackwell, 1974.

———. *Philosophical Remarks*. Oxford: Blackwell, 1975.

———. *Remarks on the Philosophy of Psychology*. Oxford: Blackwell, 1980.

INDEX